T0324277

"*The Saints' Everlasting Rest* is a classic treatise on a favorite Puritan topic: the glory of being with Christ forever. Richard Baxter not only teaches us about heaven in a manner that fans hope into flame, but he also teaches us how to meditate on heaven so that we can enjoy a foretaste of it already on earth. Tim Cooper has done us a great service in distilling Baxter's one thousand–plus pages of seventeenth-century Puritan prolixity into a small and accessible book. May this burning coal ignite a fire in many hearts today!"

Joel R. Beeke, President and Professor of Systematic Theology and Homiletics, Puritan Reformed Theological Seminary; author, *Reformed Preaching*; coauthor, *Reformed Systematic Theology*

"'Could you not watch with me one hour?' Christ's gentle correction applies to us as well when our spirit is willing but our flesh is too weak to meditate on heaven for one hour. But in this volume are corrective words from Richard Baxter that—though updated and abridged—retain their well-earned and long-standing approval. Taking us by the hand, Baxter draws us away from our egregious neglect of duty and leads us into the joy of thoughts that ring with faith, desires that ache for paradise, and disciplines that dispose us again toward the rest that Christ is preparing for us in our Father's house."

A. Craig Troxel, Professor of Practical Theology, Westminster Seminary California; author, *With All Your Heart*

The Saints' Everlasting Rest

The Saints' Everlasting Rest

Richard Baxter

Updated and Abridged by Tim Cooper

Foreword by Joni Eareckson Tada

CROSSWAY®

WHEATON, ILLINOIS

Cover design: Jordan Signer

First printing 2022

Printed in the United States of America

Hardcover ISBN: 978-1-4335-7887-8
ePub ISBN: 978-1-4335-7890-8
PDF ISBN: 978-1-4335-7888-5
Mobipocket ISBN: 978-1-4335-7889-2

Library of Congress Cataloging-in-Publication Data

Names: Baxter, Richard, 1615–1691, author. | Cooper, Tim, 1970–
Title: The saints' everlasting rest / Richard Baxter ; updated and abridged by Tim Cooper ; foreword by Joni Eareckson Tada.
Description: Updated and abridged edition. | Wheaton, Illinois : Crossway, 2022. | Includes bibliographical references and indexes.
Identifiers: LCCN 2021026067 (print) | LCCN 2021026068 (ebook) | ISBN 9781433578878 (hardcover) | ISBN 9781433578885 (pdf) | ISBN 9781433578892 (mobi) | ISBN 9781433578908 (epub)
Subjects: LCSH: Devotional literature.
Classification: LCC BV4832.3.B492 C66 2022 (print) | LCC BV4832.3.B492 (ebook) | DDC 242—dc23
LC record available at https://lccn.loc.gov/2021026067
LC ebook record available at https://lccn.loc.gov/2021026068

Crossway is a publishing ministry of Good News Publishers.

VP		31	30	29	28	27	26	25	24	23
15	14	13	12	11	10	9	8	7	6	5	4	3	2

Contents

Foreword

THE FIRST TIME I read the work of a Puritan preacher, I barely made it through the second chapter. I was told there were hidden treasures for my soul in those pages, but I lacked the mental toughness needed to break through the impenetrable text. I pushed it aside. *Shakespeare is easier than this*, I decided. At the dewy age of seventeen, so many other, more inviting and alluring paths beckoned.

Then I broke my neck, and all bets were off.

No longer could I wade in the comfortable shallows where my faith was ankle-deep. Head over heels, I had been heaved out into the depths of God, where I could not touch bottom, and I was sinking fast. *Oh God, help!*

And who, besides the Almighty himself, could begin to fathom the frightening depths in which I found myself? Yes, the psalmist tells us that "deep calls to deep" (Ps. 42:7 ESV), but where could I find those who had plumbed this Mariana Trench I was in? Could someone—anyone—show me how not to fear it but to find God in it?

Return to the Puritans, I thought. And I'm so very glad I did. From Jeremiah Burroughs, I learned to subtract my desires to fit a life of paralysis. Samuel Rutherford told me not even to think about sneaking quietly into heaven without a cross. Jonathan Edwards helped me explore that awe-filled trench, that vast, bottomless ocean of God. And Thomas Brooks said that next to Christ, I should set the choicest saints before me as a pattern for living. I did just that with the likes of these valiant, far-seeing men.

When hard suffering is your daily fare, you gravitate toward people who are deeply serious about God, life, and faith. Your spirit resonates with them. You recognize—and trust—their counsel, and you easily fall into the irresistible orb of their love for Jesus Christ. The Puritans have that inexorable pull. And it's the Puritans who beckon us beyond the shallows and into the glorious depths of God, where the inability to touch bottom never ignites fear but rather generates sheer *delight*.

Doesn't every Christian want this? Doesn't every believer want to go deep, even if it's costly? Don't we all long for and look forward to heaven? I sure do. It's not just the prospect of "setting aside this tent," as the apostle Peter put it (cf. 2 Pet. 1:14). And it's not really because I yearn to wrestle free of this confounded thing called affliction. It's more than those things. The Puritan exposition of the Bible shows how my joyous daily carrying of a cross holds a mysterious connection to a far greater joy (inexplicable and unspeakable), worship, and service of God in heaven.

Nowhere is this idea expounded more thoroughly than in Richard Baxter's timeless classic *The Saints' Everlasting Rest.* For centuries it has been lauded as the quintessential work on our heavenly rest and how we can best prepare for it. Baxter embarked on this subject while recovering from a serious illness. As he looked death full in the face, his thoughts naturally turned toward heaven. He asked himself, "What is it like? How can I prepare for it?" His study resulted in an immensely weighty book that was a spectacular bestseller in the 1600s.

Yet nowadays when you try to read the original version of *The Saints' Everlasting Rest*—even earlier abridgments—it's like paddling a canoe upstream on a swift-running river. The concepts and phrases rush at you. It's a complex, convoluted text that only a persnickety, pedantic grammar czar could love.

This is where our hero Tim Cooper boldly wades into the stream. Tim is not only professor of church history at the University of Otago in New Zealand but a renowned expert on Richard Baxter. With consummate care and expertise, Tim tackles *The Saints' Everlasting Rest* with all the respect and honor due this lauded Puritan. (And so he should, given that Baxter's contemporaries claimed their friend was in a class with the early church fathers.) Tim has performed heroic surgery on this seventeenth-century masterpiece—relieving it of the interminable sentences, semicolons, and subordinate clauses so bewildering to a modern reader.

When I read this new abridged version of Baxter's treatise, I was enthralled. Captivated. I was so invigorated, I immediately stopped and thanked God for the likes of Tim Cooper. Here is a man who possessed the mental toughness needed to break through the impenetrable language, revealing sparkling treasures such as these:

Take your heart once again and lead it by the hand. Bring it to the top of the highest mountain. Show it the kingdom of Christ and the glory of it. Say to your heart, "All this will your Lord bestow on you. . . . This is your own inheritance! This crown is yours. These pleasures are yours. This company is yours. This beauteous place is yours. All things are yours, because you are Christ's and Christ is yours." (p. 137)

Hold out a little longer, oh my soul, and bear with the infirmities of your earthly tabernacle, for soon you will rest from all your afflictions. (p. 69)

> Be up and doing; run, strive, fight, and hold on, for you have a certain glorious prize before you. (p. 70)

Heart-stirring exhortations such as these do not play well in a Christian culture that equates heaven more with end-time prophecy than a joyous rest for happy saints. Richard Baxter does not fit in a church that is quick to pray away suffering rather than embrace it as providence. Believers who are content to know little of God cannot know much of what it means to enjoy him, and so their interest in Richard Baxter is summed up in a two-line quotation shared on Instagram or Facebook.

But not me—and not many thousands like me. So if you are ready to set your heart on things above and train your affections on God, if you want to strive harder for your glorious prize and drive your heart ever onward and upward, if you feel that this is the season you finally leave the comfortable shallows of God and dive into his mysterious, wondrous depths, you could have no better guide than the remarkable work you hold in your hands.

Let the Spirit-driven exhortations in *The Saints' Everlasting Rest* explain to your heart its final home. For as our Puritan friend says,

> Oh my soul, . . . there is love in [Christ's] eyes. Listen, does he not call you? He bids you stand here at his right hand. . . .
>
> Farewell, my hard and rocky heart. Farewell, my proud and unbelieving heart. Farewell, my idolatrous and worldly heart. Farewell, my sensual and carnal heart. And now welcome, most holy and heavenly nature. . . .
>
> Ah, my drowsy, earthy, blockish heart! How coldly you think of this reviving day! Do you sleep when you think of eternal rest? Are you leaning earthward when heaven is before you? Would you

rather sit down in the dirt and dung than walk in the court of the palace of God? Come away! Make no excuse, make no delay. God commands you, and I command you: Come away! (pp. 151–52)

Oh friend, my heart leaps for joy at such an exhortation! Heaven is about to burst on the horizon, so wake up your soul, and put oil in your lamp. Join me in preparing yourself for that glorious day when we will put on sparkling raiment and ascend the throne with our bridegroom to be presented before God Almighty himself. Do not tarry one minute longer—turn the page, and begin turning your heart toward heaven, your real home.

Joni Eareckson Tada
Joni and Friends International Disability Center
Agoura Hills, California

Introduction

RICHARD BAXTER (1615–1691) was one of the most significant seventeenth-century English Puritans and certainly the most prolific. He wrote around 140 books in the course of his long life. They traverse almost every conceivable subject, from history to philosophy to theology, and they range across all aspects of Christian thought and practice. All share the Puritan concern for earnest endeavor, and all are enriched by Baxter's experience as a pastor in the parish of Kidderminster during his ministry there from 1647 to 1660. He was an author whose published works drew both notoriety and devotion. His more controversial books have been left to languish in the seventeenth century, but his "practical works" were republished in the eighteenth century and remain available online today. Among those works, two stand out above all others: *The Reformed Pastor* and *The Saints' Everlasting Rest*. They now form a matching pair of Crossway abridgments. Both abridgments seek to distill the genius of each book while rendering Baxter's language in contemporary English. The aim is to allow modern readers to encounter these two classic works in a fresh and accessible way.

The Saints' Everlasting Rest has been republished again and again since it first appeared in 1650.[1] In Baxter's day it had reached eight editions by 1659 and twelve editions by 1688; we would call it a runaway

---

1   For an account of the book's reception, see Keith Condie, "The Theory, Practice, and Reception of Meditation in the Thought of Richard Baxter" (PhD diss., University

bestseller. Many readers sent letters of approval to the author. From all the way across the Atlantic in 1656, for example, the early American missionary John Eliot thanked Baxter for the book: "Oh, what a sweet refreshing the Lord made it to be unto me, especially when I came to that blessed point and pattern of holy meditation." Baxter, he observed, had "a rare gift, especially to follow a meditation to the very end, bring it to an issue, and set it forth for a pattern."[2] Nearer to home, the Wiltshire minister Peter Ince wrote to say, "I do not know of any book that the Lord has made more use of for rousing up men to an active faith than yours."[3]

In focusing on heaven, *The Saints' Everlasting Rest* clearly touched a nerve and met a need. The book's broad success may have had something to do with the tumultuous quality of England's history during Baxter's lifetime: civil war, the execution of the king, the formation of a republic, the restoration of the monarchy, the persecution of Puritan Nonconformity, and the "Glorious Revolution." In times of such upheaval, who would not welcome a message of our eternal rest? And ever since then, the book has been in print almost continuously as a stand-alone work. There is something about its heart, its insight, that justifies its continued availability. It can speak to our own day just as well as to Baxter's. But to grasp the book's compelling quality, we need to understand the context in which he first began to write.

---

   of Sydney, 2010), chap. 4. This dissertation also offers an excellent examination of Baxter's practice of meditation.

2 John Eliot to Richard Baxter, October 16, 1656, Baxter Correspondence, vol. 3, folio 7r, Dr. Williams's Library. As in the abridged text, I have modernized the language in all the quotations in this introduction.

3 Peter Ince to Richard Baxter, November 16, 1652, Baxter Correspondence, vol. 4, folio 181r, Dr. Williams's Library.

Baxter's War

England was torn apart by civil war during the 1640s. The conflict emerged from tensions over political liberties, constitutional prerogatives, financial pressures, and, above all, religious differences. King Charles I imposed on the Church of England a distinctive vision of deference and order along with a new demand for uniformity of practice. The result was a heavily sacramental and liturgical style of worship that minimized the place of preaching and Scripture in the corporate life of the church. Charles and his archbishop of Canterbury, William Laud, actively sidelined Calvinist doctrine with its focus on God's effectual saving grace in predestination and election to promote in its place a doctrine of salvation that valued human free will and moral responsibility. It all looked worryingly Roman Catholic at a time when the Protestant Reformation seemed to be in retreat on the continent of Europe.

When the Irish Catholics rebelled in 1641, with rumors that the king himself had sanctioned their revolt, Parliament took control of the various militias organized to put down the uprising. In October 1642 actual fighting broke out between Parliament's forces and those of the king, the beginning of four years of bitter military conflict that ranged across the entire country and, in later phases, even into Scotland and Ireland. The destruction was immense and widespread, the loss of life brutal. It is estimated that in the course of those wars, 868,000 people died in battle or were brought down by disease across all three countries, more than 10 percent of the total population.[4]

The 1640s, then, presented England with a grievous trauma on a national scale. That trauma was mirrored in the experience of countless

---

4   Charles Carlton, *Going to the Wars: The Experience of the British Civil Wars, 1638–1651* (London: Routledge, 1992), 214.

individuals, not least Richard Baxter. In an uncanny combination of circumstances, he was present to witness the first physical skirmish of the war, an impromptu ambush of parliamentary soldiers.[5] He was also on hand to see for himself the mournful aftereffects of the first full battle of the war, fought at Edgehill precisely one month later. He visited the battlefield the following day, where he saw "about a thousand dead bodies in the field between the two forces, and I suppose many more buried before."[6] He offered no comment on the grisly sight, but it must have been a harrowing scene. Baxter was intimately familiar with the grim reality of the war from the very beginning.

At this stage in his life, he was embarking on a period of itinerancy, having been thrust out of his fledgling pastoral ministry at Kidderminster "by the insurrection of a rabble that with clubs sought to kill me."[7] The Midlands lay in Royalist territory, which was hardly welcome terrain for a Puritan such as Baxter, so he spent the next few years living in Coventry ministering to the garrison stationed in the city. In July 1645 he signed up as an army chaplain in an effort to combat the spread of bad doctrine in the army. He joined the regiment of Colonel Edward Whalley as it traversed the country fighting the last battles against the king and laying siege to several sites of lingering resistance. At the start of 1647, just as the winter reached its coldest point, his nose started to bleed. In the medical wisdom of the day, this was taken to represent an excess of blood, so he opened four veins,

---

5 Richard Baxter, *Reliquiae Baxterianae: Or, Mr. Richard Baxter's Narrative of the Most Memorable Passages of His Life and Times*, ed. Matthew Sylvester (London, 1696), 1.42, §60.

6 Baxter, *Reliquiae Baxterianae*, 1.43, §61.

7 Richard Baxter to Stephen Lobb, June 9, 1684, Baxter Correspondence, vol. 2, folio 93r, Dr. Williams's Library.

followed by another more substantial purge. This drastic loss of blood very nearly killed him.[8] As he explained in a letter to a friend that he wrote at the time, "I was never yet nearly so low, . . . and if I see your face no more in the flesh, farewell till eternity." His only hope lay in prayer: "There is no other hope left: physicians, nature, flesh, blood, spirit, heart, friends all fail. But God is the strength of my heart and my portion forever."[9] He was quoting Psalm 73:26, which appeared on the title page to *The Saints' Everlasting Rest* (see fig. 1).

Indeed, the crisis may have ended Baxter's work as an army chaplain, but it triggered his writing career. As he started a slow recovery, now aged thirty-one, he began to write what he initially intended as his funeral sermon, presumably a gathering of his final thoughts to preach to himself. Those thoughts steadily grew into *The Saints' Everlasting Rest*: what you have in your hands is therefore a compressed version of Baxter's dying words, even if he lived for another forty-five years. As he explained when he dedicated the book to his beloved parishioners at Kidderminster, it was "written, as it were, by a man who was between living and dead." In that condition, "far from home, cast into extreme languishing by the sudden loss of about a gallon of blood, I bent my thoughts on my everlasting rest."[10] His book urges us to do the same, to turn our minds toward heaven and the prospect of our rest in the presence of God after a weary pilgrimage through this dismal world.

---

8 Baxter, *Reliquiae Baxterianae*, 1.58, §85.

9 Richard Baxter to an unnamed friend, February 1647, in Don Gilbert, *"Undeserved Mercies": The Life of Richard Baxter (1615–1691)* (Kidderminster: Don Gilbert, 2016), 171.

10 Richard Baxter, *The Saints' Everlasting Rest: Or, A Treatise of the Blessed State of the Saints and Their Enjoyment of God in Glory* (London, 1650), dedication of the whole, sig. A2v.

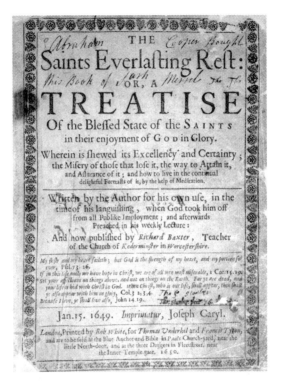

Figure 1   Original title page of *The Saints' Everlasting Rest*. Used by permission of Dr. Williams's Library, London.

And Baxter's world had been dismal. As he explained to Colonel Whalley in a letter of 1654, "The memory of those [war] years is so little delightful to me that I look back on them as the saddest of my life."[11] *The Saints' Everlasting Rest* may focus the mind on heaven, but there is no avoiding the bleak reality of Baxter's earthly experience

---

11 Richard Baxter to Edward Whalley, March 8, 1653, in Richard Baxter, *Richard Baxter's Apology against the Modest Exceptions of Mr T. Blake* (London, 1654), 2v.

at a time of turmoil, devastation, and crisis on both a personal and a national scale. Thus the Civil Wars intrude into his book again and again. In one extended lament, he observes the "days of common suffering when nothing appears to our sight but ruin: families ruined, congregations ruined, sumptuous structures ruined, cities ruined, country ruined, court ruined, and kingdoms ruined" (p. 67). He recalls "the sad and heart-piercing spectacles that my eyes have seen in four years of civil war: in this fight a dear friend falls down by me; from another battle a precious Christian is brought home wounded or dead; scarcely a month, hardly a week without the sight or noise of war" (pp. 67–68). We might take a moment to reflect on what it would have been like for him to live through two years of horror on a regular basis. He surely had in mind the grisly tableau at Edgehill when he looked forward to that time when, as he said, "my eyes will never more behold the earth covered with the carcasses of the slain" (p. 68). Thus Baxter emerged from the wars with a lingering sense of trauma that infiltrates *The Saints' Everlasting Rest*, even as his book points toward an eternal future of commanding joy and rest.

Baxter's Method

Despite the severity of his near-death encounter in the winter of 1647, Baxter was grateful for it. That experience, he recalled, "forced me to that work of meditation that I had formerly found so profitable to my soul."[12] It would seem, then, that meditation had been a regular practice for him, now perhaps more intensely focused on the prospect of his imminent heavenly rest. As he developed his book, he intended to bring the reader into a new resolve to practice this

---

12 Baxter, *Saints' Everlasting Rest* (1650), dedication of the whole, sig. A2v.

"work of meditation." The method he pioneered for himself he now enjoined on his audience, and he does not call it a "work" for nothing. For Baxter, meditation was not merely the passing of some fleeting thoughts through the mind as the occasion arises. It involved focus and effort; it was determined, intentional, structured, deliberate, and regular; it embodied what he called the "great duty of a heavenly life" (p. 108). There were many hindrances in its way, particularly in the sluggish workings and perverse reluctance of the human heart. In his experience, it was a rare Christian who practiced daily meditation on heaven. But the effort brought great gain for those who would make it their own. He had proved that for himself.

Baxter's method was grounded in a tripartite understanding of the nature of each human person: judgment, will, and affections. Christian truths were inadequate if they resided only in the mind, or the judgment. The will had to be brought into play to move those divine truths from the judgment into the affections, from the head to the heart. The main way of doing this was through soliloquy, or "preaching to oneself" (p. 150). Centuries before the development of modern psychological theories, Baxter intuited the power in the way we talk to ourselves. His other word for this self-talk is "consideration," which "opens the door between the head and the heart" (p. 130). Consideration is a reasoning with oneself. His method of meditation involves us in coaxing our own hearts with sufficient reasons to move our affections. With time, effort, and resolve, our emotions begin to answer, we feel the force of those truths, and our hearts are lifted up in love, desire, hope, courage, and joy (chap. 10). The crucial element in achieving these gains is how we talk to ourselves. One of the most compelling and endearing aspects of the book is that Baxter increasingly allows us into his own mind to hear for ourselves how this great

Puritan spoke to himself. The final chapter provides an exemplar of his own meditation. *The Saints' Everlasting Rest* is a personal gift of the most intimate kind.

Baxter's method was also grounded in the conviction that God does not work mysteriously, as if by magic; he works by means, and those means are at our disposal. "Man is a rational creature and apt to be moved in a reasoning way" (p. 130). Each of us is capable of using our own God-given faculties to bring divine truths home to our heart: "Must not everything first enter your judgment and consideration before it can delight your heart and affection? God does his work on us as men and in a rational way. He enables and energizes us to consider and study these delightful objects and thus to gather our own comforts as the bee gathers honey from the flowers" (p. 97). Just as bees work hard and work methodically to gather their honey, so too, Christians are to work in the way God has designed them to work. He "enables and energizes us," but there is no honey without our own cooperation. "You will enjoy God only as much as you train your understanding and affections sincerely on him" (p. 121).

Much of the book carries Baxter's reflections on what the saints' experience of heaven will be like. With a richness of texture and imagination, Baxter weaves together scriptural signposts with his thoughtful impressions of what the future might hold when we will be fully alive at last in the presence of God. He also impresses on us how our present life must necessarily change if we genuinely take that prospect to be true. This is his manifesto for how we are to live and how we are to die—on a daily basis. Baxter's challenging insights become a succession of wedges that pry our attachments away from the pleasures and comforts, the customs and values of this world. His deep impressions could only have come from extended reflection on heaven. They are the product of his method, and he invites us into the same practice of daily meditation that generated those insights. There is an urgent authenticity to his book. In those dismal days of civil war, he set his sights firmly on heaven. In these more comfortable times, four centuries later, he challenges us to do the same. Do you really believe in heaven? Reading this book will put that belief to the test.

But if we are prepared to put in the work of daily meditation, we will reap a rich reward. As Baxter explains in the book's conclusion, "Be acquainted with this work, and you will, in some small, remote way, be acquainted with God. Your joys will be spiritual, prevalent, and lasting, according to the nature of their blessed object" (160). Those joys will bring great gain even in the worst of circumstances.

> You will have comfort in life and comfort in death. When you have neither wealth, nor health, nor the pleasure of this world, yet you will have comfort: a comfort without the presence or help of any friend, without a minister, without a book; when all means are denied you or taken from you, even then you may have vigorous, real comfort. (p. 160)

To pilgrims on a journey through a dark and painful world, such comfort will be welcome indeed.

Baxter's World

But is the world as dark as all that? Very few, if any, contemporary readers of this book will find themselves in the middle of a vicious civil war. We live in a historical moment of relative comfort, safety, and affluence; is Baxter's experience going to speak to our own? Throughout the book he talks a lot about happiness, but it is not reassuring when he claims that "happiness is hereafter, and not here."[13] In other words, happiness is something we should look for only in heaven; we should not expect to find it or even seek it here on earth. This is not our home; here we only get by. "This world," he says, "is a howling wilderness," and "most of the inhabitants are untamed, hideous monsters" (p. 156). We are soldiers in the midst of battle, sailors still seeking safe harbor, and travelers making our weary way home. Only then will we rest. In the meantime, our earthly life is filled with labor and travail, and we should expect no less. This is, to say the least, a bleak perspective.

It is worth noting that Baxter had other reasons to be weary of this world that had nothing to do with civil war, and perhaps these other dimensions will resonate more with our own experience. To begin with, he battled ill health his whole life long. He was, in the apt words of Neil Keeble, "subject to a bewildering variety of physical ailments."[14] To name a few: kidney stones; pain in his eyes, teeth, jaws, and joints; and what he described as "incredible inflammations of my stomach, bowels, back, sides, head, and thighs."[15] As he explained in a 1649 letter, "If I have any ease one day, I am sick another. I can scarcely remember two hours together for the past two years when I have been free from pain in one part of my body or another, except sleeping."[16]

13 Baxter, *Saints' Everlasting Rest* (1650), 74.
14 Neil Keeble, *Richard Baxter: Puritan Man of Letters*, Oxford English Monographs (Oxford: Clarendon, 1982), 11.
15 Baxter, *Reliquiae Baxterianae*, 3.173, §311.
16 Richard Baxter to John Warren, September 11, 1649, Baxter Correspondence, vol. 6, folio 96r, Dr. Williams's Library.

Inevitably, this extended sickness and chronic pain also makes its way into his book. He writes of "one like myself, who, in the last ten or twelve years, has barely had a whole day free from some pain or discomfort. Oh, the weary nights and days! Oh, the tedious, nauseous medicines! Is it not desirable to rest from all these?" (p. 68). In such pain and discomfort, no wonder he yearned for a future rest from all his troubles. We might do the same.

Baxter's experience also gave him other reasons to view this earthly pilgrimage with a jaundiced eye, experience in which we all can surely share. There is the encounter with our own sinfulness, for a start, that confronts us every day: "We can barely open our eyes, and we are in danger" (p. 66). Thus the church, he says, is like a hospital filled with groaning patients. Some Christians "are weary of a blind mind with its doubts concerning the way they walk; they are unsettled in almost all their thoughts. Some are weary of a hard heart, some of a proud heart, some of a passionate heart, and some are weary of all of these" (pp. 58–59). We also encounter variability and change as we move through our life; we are buffeted about by winds from all directions. "We wonder at those changes of Providence toward us, being scarcely two days together in the same condition. Today we are well, and we conclude that the bitterness of death is past; tomorrow we are sick and conclude that we will shortly perish by our illness. Today we are in esteem, tomorrow in disgrace; today we have friends, tomorrow none; today we are in gladness, tomorrow in sadness" (p. 61). Put in these terms, the prospect of everlasting, unchanging rest sounds more and more appealing. There is an awful lot to rest from.

If we think that Baxter is too gloomy about our current existence, we might also bear in mind that he has Scripture as his starting point. Peter addresses us as "sojourners and exiles" (1 Pet. 2:11 ESV). Paul reminds us that "our citizenship is in heaven" (Phil. 3:20 ESV). The writer to the Hebrews presents us with those heroes of faith who "acknowledged that they were strangers and exiles on the earth," who demonstrated by hard choices that "they desire[d] a better country, that is, a heavenly one" (Heb. 11:13, 16 ESV). Above all, the same writer declares that "there remains a Sabbath rest for the people of God" (Heb. 4:9 ESV). *The Saints' Everlasting Rest* is an extended sermon or reflection on the implications of just that one verse. This world is not our home; here we will find no true rest. We might say that Baxter takes this insight too far, that he dismisses too comprehensively the prospect of genuine happiness in this life and not just in the life to come. Even so, given the current Western culture of comfort, entertainment, and celebrity, perhaps that is a caution we need to hear. He may be more properly oriented to the voice of Scripture than we are.

But if happiness is thin on the ground in Baxter's world, joy is still to be found. Indeed, it is one of the main benefits of his method. "That which will make us most happy when we possess it will make us most joyful when we meditate on it" (p. 122). Joy is the reward for those who will take Baxter at his word and practice his method of daily meditation on our future rest. "You will find that there is indeed sweetness in the work and way of God and that the life of Christianity is a life of joy" (p. 96). The practice of daily meditation is the key. "A heavenly mind is a joyful mind. This is the nearest and truest way to live a life of comfort; without this, you must necessarily be uncomfortable" (p. 96).

Baxter's Book

All these themes weave their way through *The Saints' Everlasting Rest*. The book begins with Baxter's conception of what that rest will look like and feel like. He describes the future, particularly the way we will enter into our rest—through the inevitable doorway of physical death. He celebrates all those things we will rest from. He supplies us with no fewer than fifty reasons to focus our minds on this rest. He challenges our reluctance to pass through death when such a glorious rest awaits us on the other side and when we will leave behind such a dismal existence as this one. "Oh foolish, unworthy soul, who would rather wander in this land of darkness, in this barren wilderness, than be at rest with Jesus Christ!" (p. 91). He lists the gains to be made from meditating on our heavenly rest, and he points out what will help us and what will get in the way. Having laid this solid foundation, he then proceeds to instruct us in his method of meditation. Finally, he demonstrates that method for us by allowing us to hear how he talked to himself. "Though he died, he still speaks" (Heb. 11:4 ESV).

In the original book, Baxter did all this in exhaustive length. The first edition of 1650 comprised 853 pages and around 350,000 words. This abridgment is a tenth of that, at around 35,000 words. It complements my abridgment of *The Reformed Pastor*, and I have gone about my task in much the same way. I have tried to distill the essence of a book that is long, complex, daunting, and unwieldy, even if it remains a work of enduring genius and relevance. This edition is much simpler, cleaner, and clearer. My goal is to do justice to what Baxter wanted to say in *The Saints' Everlasting Rest* while still being readable, accessible, and manageable for the contemporary reader.

There are a few dimensions that I have simply left out. The original work devoted around one hundred pages to defending the truth of Scripture, and it contained several long passages on assurance of salvation. Both of these aspects are somewhat removed from Baxter's central line of thought and are expressed in seventeenth-century arguments we will not find so compelling today. I have also omitted a number of controversies that he felt compelled to notice along the way but will be of little interest to us now. Otherwise, I have tried to encompass the breadth of Baxter's project in a way that is still faithful to him, if a great deal shorter.

I have taken a number of liberties with the text without making any of them obvious. If Baxter has already made his point earlier, I have sought to minimize repetition. If I have felt that he has made his point sufficiently in the first half of a long paragraph, I have quite happily omitted the second half, or I have retained what I think are the most pertinent, affecting, and accessible of his sentences and deleted the rest. I have reorganized and occasionally reordered the chapters. I have split many long sentences in two; amended Baxter's heavy use of colons, semicolons, and commas; modernized his rather random placement of apostrophes; and used contemporary spelling. I have inserted new words to ease the flow from one sentence to another or shifted a clause from the end of a long sentence to the beginning. I have also amended all those tiny archaic constructions that snag the eye and get in the way, lower-cased the initial capital letter in many of the nouns, and replaced unfamiliar, ancient terms with their contemporary equivalents. And I have modernized seventeenth-century verb endings (e.g., *hath*, *hindereth*). (See fig. 2 for a glimpse of Baxter's writing from a page in the original.) Even so, there is a residual strangeness to his writing. His distinctive construction of written English is a useful reminder that, for all the many continuities, Baxter lived in a world far different from our own. For this reason, I have not updated his gendered language.

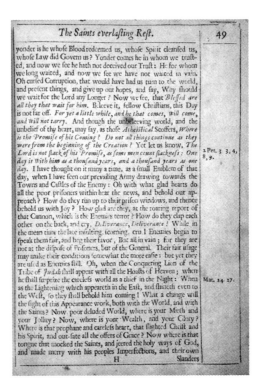

Figure 2   A page from the original publication of *The Saints'*
Everlasting Rest. For the equivalent text in this edition, see pp.
45–46. Used by permission of Dr. Williams's Library, London.

The book should, then, be entirely accessible and familiar, and yet
its central idea is strikingly unfamiliar. The thought of actively, intentionally, and daily meditating on our heavenly rest is nearly unheard
of today. If that is the case, little has changed across the centuries.
This practice of meditation offers abundant consolation, but in his
own time Baxter lamented that "so few Christians ever here obtain

[that consolation] because they do not know this way or walk in it" (p. 96). What Baxter urges on us with such intensity may seem novel, quaint, and unnecessary. But be warned. He will confront you with a challenge that you cannot ignore, and he will demand an answer. So I leave the final words to Baxter, words that you will soon encounter again: "Reader, stop here while you answer my question. . . . What do you say—yes or no? . . . [A]re you willing, or are you not? Will you obey if I show you the way of your duty? May the Lord persuade your heart to the work" (p. 104).

Tim Cooper
Dunedin, New Zealand

1

What This Rest Contains

In this chapter Baxter begins to unfold his vision of what our experience of heaven will be like. Finally we will be free from sin and evil, perfect in all our capacities, and full to overflowing with the love of God and the joyous delight of being in his intimate presence. In painting this picture, Baxter draws a stark contrast between the saints' experience in heaven and the dismal daily reality they face here on earth.

IT WAS NOT ONLY our interest in God and our joyful possession of him that was lost in Adam's fall but all spiritual knowledge of God and a true disposition toward such a happiness. Man now has a heart too suitable to his estate: a low state and a low spirit. So when the Son of God comes with recovering grace to offer a spiritual and eternal happiness and glory, he does not find faith in man to believe it (Luke 18:8). We are like the poor man who would not believe that anyone had such a sum as a hundred pounds because it was so far beyond what he ever possessed. We are like the Israelites: When God gave them his Sabbaths of rest in a land of rest, he had more work to do to make them believe it than he had to overcome their enemies and obtain it for them. Then when they had it, though it was only as a small intimation of a more incomparably glorious rest through Christ, they simply sat down and said, "Surely there's no other heaven but this." In a similar way, we hardly believe that there is such a happiness as Christ has obtained for us.

The writer to the Hebrews devotes most of his letter to addressing this disorder. He clearly and expansively proves that the end of all ceremonies and shadows is in Jesus Christ, the substance. He demonstrates that the rest of Sabbaths and Canaan should teach his Christian readers to look for a further rest, which indeed is their happiness: "There remains therefore a rest for the people of God" (Heb. 4:9). This text is his conclusion after various arguments to that end, and it remains a useful conclusion for the believer today. It contains the ground of all his comforts, the end of all his duty and sufferings, and the life and sum of all gospel promises and Christian privileges. Thus you may easily see why I have made this verse the subject of this book. What could be more welcome to men under personal afflictions, tiring duty, and a succession of sufferings than rest? What could supply more welcome news to men under public calamities, unpleasing employments, plundering, losses, and all sorts of sad tidings than this news of rest? Reader, I pray to God that your attentions, intention of spirit, reception, and improvement of this welcome news will be even half answerable to the truth, necessity, and excellency of the subject. Then you will have cause to bless God while you live that ever you heard it.

A Perfect End

I will begin by describing what is contained in this Sabbath rest that remains for the people of God. First of all, this rest contains a cessation from all motion or action that implies the absence of the end.

When we have reached the harbor, we have finished sailing. When the workman has his wages, he has completed his work. All motion ends at the center, and all means cease when we have the end. Thus there will be no more prayer, because there will be no more necessity, only the full enjoyment of what we prayed for. We will not need to fast, weep, and watch anymore, being out of the reach of sin and temptations. Nor will we need instruction and exhortation: preaching is done; ministry ceases; the sacraments are now past their use. The laborers are called in because the harvest is gathered; the tares are burnt, and the work is done (Matt. 13:24–30). The unregenerate are past hope; the saints are past fear forever.

This rest contains a perfect freedom from all the evils that accompanied us through our course in this world, for nothing enters heaven that defiles or is unclean (Rev. 21:27). Doubtless, there is no such thing as grief and sorrow there. Nor is there such a thing as a pale face, feeble joints, languishing sickness, groaning fears, consuming cares, or whatever deserves the name of evil. A gale of groans and a stream of tears will accompany us to the very gates, and there they will bid us farewell forever. Our sorrow will be turned into joy, and no one will take our joy from us.

This rest contains the highest degree of the saints' personal perfection, both of soul and of body, which qualifies them to enjoy the full sweetness of glory. Here, eye has not seen, nor ear heard, nor heart conceived what God has laid up for those who wait for him (1 Cor. 2:9). For the eye of flesh is not capable of seeing it, nor this ear of hearing it, nor this heart of understanding it. But there the eye, the ear, and the heart are made capable. The more perfect our sight, the more delightful the beautiful object. The more perfect our appetite, the sweeter the food. The more musical our ear, the more pleasant the melody. So too, the more perfect our soul, the more joyous those joys, and the more glorious to us is that glory.

This rest contains as the highest part our deepest enjoyment of God the highest good. And here, reader, do not be surprised if I am at a loss. When I know so little of God, I cannot know much of what it is to enjoy him. When I know so little of my own soul while it is here in this tabernacle, how little can I know of the infinite majesty or the state of this soul when it is advanced to that enjoyment? We will never be capable of clearly knowing until we are capable of fully enjoying. How can a man born blind conceive of the sun and its light? How can a man born deaf conceive of the nature of sound and music? So too, we lack still that sense by which God must be clearly known. I stand and look on a heap of ants and see them all with one view, very busy to little purpose. They do not know me, my being, nature, or thoughts, though I am their fellow creature. How little then must we know of the great Creator, though he with one view continually beholds us all? What knowledge we have is imperfect and such as must be done away with; it is only a glimpse the saints behold, as though through a glass darkly (1 Cor. 13:9–10, 12). But, poor Christian, be of good cheer. The time is near when God and you will be near, as near as you can ever desire.

Perfect Capacities

This rest also contains a sweet and constant action of all the powers of the soul and body in the joyful possession of God. First, our senses are perfected. As the ore is cast into the fire in the form of stone but comes forth as a metal so pure that it deserves another name, so much greater will be the change of our bodies and senses. We will then say, "This is not the body I had, and these are not the senses I had." But because we have no other name for them, let us continue to call them senses—call them eyes and ears, call this seeing and hearing. But observe the difference between them. This spiritual body exceeds even the glory of the sun in surpassing these frail, disagreeable, diseased lumps of flesh or dirt we now carry about us. We must conceive the change of the senses in proportion to the change of the body. As God advances our sense and enlarges our capacity, so will he advance the happiness of those senses and fill up with himself all that capacity. And if the body will be thus employed, oh, how will the soul be taken up? As its powers and capacities are greatest, so its action is strongest and its enjoyment sweetest.

Doubtless our memory will not be idle or useless in this blessed work. If it is just by looking back to help the soul to value its enjoyment, our knowledge will be enlarged, not diminished. Therefore, the knowledge of things past will not be taken away. No doubt from the height of that great mountain, the saint can look behind him and before him. To compare past with present things must surely raise in the soul an inconceivable esteem and sense of its blessed condition. To stand at that height where we can see the wilderness and Canaan both at once, to stand in heaven and look back on earth and weigh them together in the balance, how that must transport the soul!

That soul will cry out, "Is this the purchase that cost such a price as the blood of God? No wonder! Oh, blessed price and thrice-blessed love that so condescended to me! Have the gales of grace blown me into such a harbor? Is this the glory that the Scriptures spoke of and ministers preached so much of? Now I see that the gospel indeed is good tidings. Have my mourning, my fasting, my heavy walking, my groaning, and my complaints all come to this? Have all my afflictions, sickness, languishing, and fears of death come to this? Have all Satan's temptations and the world's scorns and jeers come to this? Oh, vile nature that resisted so much and so long such a blessing as this!"

That soul will look back with astonishment at the flesh that demanded to be pleased, even at the loss of this happiness. "Did you make me question the truth of this glory? Did you draw me to distrust the Lord? Did you question the truth of the Scripture that promised this rest? Well, my soul, are you not now ashamed that you ever questioned the love that has brought you here? You suspected his love when you should only have suspected yourself. Now you are convinced that the ways you called hard and the cup you called bitter were necessary. Your Lord intended sweeter ends than you would believe. Your Redeemer was saving you just as much when he crossed your desires as when he granted them, just as much when he broke your heart as when he bound it up. Oh, no thanks to you, unworthy self, but shame, for this crown you have received. But to Jehovah and the Lamb be glory forever."

Perfect Love

Love is of the essence of the soul and the essence of God, for God is love (1 John 4:8). The Spirit's phrase is "God is love, and he who dwells in love dwells in God, and God in him" (1 John 4:16). The acting of this affection carries much delight along with it, especially when the object appears deserving and the affection is strong. So what will it be like when perfected affections will have the strongest, perfect, unceasing actings on the most perfect object, the ever-blessed God?

What a great favor it is that God will give us leave to love him, that he will graciously allow himself to be embraced by such arms that have embraced lust and sin before him. But this is not all! He returns love for love, no, a thousand times more. As perfect as we will be, we cannot reach his measure of love. Christian, you will then be brimful of love, and though you love him as much as you can, you will be ten thousand times more beloved. Do you think you can overlove him? Can you love more than Love itself? The arms of the Son of God were laid wide open on the cross, and a passage was made to his heart by the spear, and will his arms and heart not be open to you in glory? Did he begin to love before you loved him (1 John 4:10, 19), and will he not continue now? Did he not love you while you were an enemy and a sinner (Rom. 5:6, 8), while you even loathed yourself? Will he not now immeasurably love you as a son, as a perfect saint, and as one who now returns pure love for his love?

Here is the saints' enjoyment and possession of God! It consists in these sweet, mutual, constant actions of love. To love and be beloved: this is our refuge in the everlasting arms (Deut. 33:27). His left hand is under our heads, and with his right hand he embraces us (Song 2:6). Reader, stop and think for a moment what a state this will be. Is it a small thing in your eyes to be beloved of God, to be the son, the spouse, the love, and the delight of the King of glory? Christian, believe this, and think on it: You will be eternally embraced in the arms of that love that is from everlasting to everlasting, of that love that brought the Son of God's love from heaven to earth, from earth to the cross, from the cross to the grave, from the grave to glory. This is the same love that was weary, hungry, tempted, scorned, scourged, buffeted, spit upon, crucified, and pierced. This is the love that fasted, prayed, taught, healed, wept, sweated, bled, and died. This is the love that will eternally embrace you. Oh, the blessed meeting when perfect created love and most perfect uncreated love meet together!

Know this, believer, to your everlasting comfort, that if these arms have once embraced you, neither sin nor hell can ever pluck you from them (John 10:28–29). The sanctuary is inviolable and the rock impregnable to which you have fled. You are safely locked up for all eternity. You no longer have to deal with a shifting, unfaithful, inconstant creature but with him in whom there is no varying nor shadow of change, even the immutable God (James 1:17). If your happiness lay in your own hand, as in Adam's, there would still be room to fear, but it is in the keeping of a faithful Creator. Christ has not bought you at so dear a price to trust you with yourself anymore. His love to you will not be as yours was on earth to him: seldom and cold, up and down, mixed with burning and quaking, with a good day and a bad. No, Christian, he who would not be discouraged by your enmity, by your loathsome, hateful nature, by all your unwillingness, unkind neglect, and grudging resistance, will not cease to love you now that he has made you truly lovely. Indeed, you may be as confident as Paul was before you that neither death nor life, nor angels nor principalities nor powers, nor things present nor things to come, nor height nor depth, nor any other creature, will be able to separate you from the love of God that is in Christ Jesus our Lord (Rom. 8:38–39).

Perfect Joy

The affection of joy will not have the least share in this possession of God. All the rest lead to and conclude in this, even the inconceivable pleasure and satisfaction that the blessed saints will feel in seeing, knowing, loving, and being beloved of God. Oh, what joy that will be when we are perfectly prepared for joy and that joy is perfectly prepared by Christ. We will make it our work and our business eternally to rejoice. Our joy is the joy of our Lord, and we will enter his joy (Matt. 25:21, 23). The same glory that the Father gives to the Son, the

Son will give to them (John 17:22). We will sit with him on his throne, even as he sat down on his Father's throne (Rev. 3:21).

What do you say to all this, you sad and drooping soul, you who now spend your days in sorrow, your breath in sighs, and who turn all your words into groaning? You know no garments but sackcloth, no food but the bread and water of affliction (Isa. 30:20). You mingle your bread with tears and drink the tears that you weep (Ps. 80:5). What do you say to this great change from all sorrow to more than all joy? You poor soul, who now prays for joy, waits for joy, complains for lack of joy, and longs for joy: behold, then you will have full joy, as much as you can hold and more than you ever conceived or your heart desired.

Oh, blessed morning, thrice-blessed morning! Poor, humble, drooping soul, how would it fill you with joy now if a voice from heaven were to tell you of the love of God to you? The angels will bring you to Christ, and Christ will take you by the hand and lead you into the purchased possession, bid you welcome to his rest, present you unspotted before his Father (Jude 1:24), and give you your place about his throne. Poor sinner, what do you say to such a day as this? Will you not be almost ready to draw back and say, "What, me, Lord? Me, the unworthy neglecter of your grace who so slighted your love? Should I have this glory? Make me a hired servant; I am not worthy to be called a son" (cf. Luke 15:19). But Love will have it so; therefore, you must enter into his joy.

Yes, the Father himself puts on joy as well, in our joy. Oh, how quickly even now he spies the returning prodigal, even from afar. He runs and meets him; he falls with compassion on his neck and kisses him. He puts the best robe around him, a ring on his finger, and shoes on his feet. He does not spare the fatted calf, that they may eat and be merry (Luke 15:20–23). That was indeed a merry meeting, but it is nothing to the embracing and the joy of that last and great meeting.

Questions for Reflection

1. Baxter's key text is Hebrews 4:9: "There remains therefore a rest for the people of God." What do you think that verse means? Is Baxter right to look for the fulfillment of this rest in heaven?

2. Heaven occupies a great deal of Baxter's thoughts. How much does heaven occupy your thoughts? Does this world take up too much of your affections and attention?

3. What difference might it make to your life if you developed the same consciousness of heaven that Baxter demonstrates? What do you think it would take for you to cultivate the same kind of daily awareness of your eternal future?

4. What aspects of Baxter's vision of heaven do you particularly notice or appreciate?

The Four Corners of This Portico

How will the saints enter their rest? If heaven is like a temple, they must enter through the portico, which has four corners or stages: Christ will return to take his people to be with himself, their bodies will be resurrected, they will pass through the judgment without fear or condemnation, and they will be crowned with Christ and sit with him on his throne. Death is a necessary part of this entrance into everlasting rest, but it is by no means to be feared.

IN THE FIRST CHAPTER, I opened a window toward the temple and showed you only the smallest glimpse of the saints' everlasting rest. Now let us proceed to view a little of the blessed properties of this rest. For the portico of this temple is exceedingly glorious, and its gate is called Beautiful (Acts 3:2). I will briefly unfold for you the four corners of this portico: Christ's return, our resurrection, our judgment, and our coronation. Follow this fourfold stream to its head, and it will bring you to the garden of Eden.

Christ's Return

This is most clear: Christ will come again to receive his people to himself, so that where he is, there they may be also (John 14:3). The bridegroom's departure was not a divorce. He did not leave intending to return no more. And he has left pledges enough to assure us: we have his word; his many promises; his sacraments, which show forth his death until he comes; and his Spirit, to direct, sanctify, and comfort us until he returns. We have frequent tokens of love from him to show us that he does not forget his promise or us. Therefore, let the saints lift up their heads, for their redemption draws near.

Imagine, fellow Christian, what would we do if our Lord did not intend to return? What misfortune! But will he really leave us among wolves (Acts 20:29), in the lions' den (Dan. 6), among a generation of serpents (Matt. 23:33), and here forget us? Would he buy us at so dear a price (1 Cor. 6:20) and then cast us off? Will he leave us sinning, suffering, groaning, dying daily, and come no more to us? It cannot be! Never fear: it cannot be. That would be like how we deal with Christ. When we feel ourselves warm and comfortable in the world, we hardly care about coming to him. But this is not like Christ's dealing with us. He who came to suffer will surely come to triumph. He who came to purchase will surely come to possess. Where else could we place all our hopes? What would become of our faith, our prayers, our tears, and our waiting? What would all the patience of the saints be worth to them? Would we not be left of all men the most miserable (1 Cor. 15:19)? Reader, consider that Christ has called us to forsake all the world and be forsaken by all the world—and all this for him, so that we might have him instead of all. Do you really think that he will, after all this, forget us and forsake us himself? Far be such a thought from our hearts!

Oh fellow Christian, what a day that will be, when we who have been kept prisoners by sin, by sinners, and by the grave will be fetched out by the Lord himself. Christ will surely come from heaven to conquer his enemies and set his captives free. It will not be like his first coming, in poverty and contempt. He will not come to be spit upon, buffeted, scorned, and crucified again. He will not come, oh careless world, to be slighted and neglected by you anymore. Yet even his first coming, which was necessarily in infirmity and reproach for our sakes, did not lack its own glory. The angels of heaven brought tidings of joy to all people, and the heavenly host praised God with that solemnity, "Glory to God in the highest, and on earth peace and goodwill toward men" (Luke 2:14).

Believe it, fellow Christians, this day is not far off. For in just a little while, he who comes will come and will not delay (Heb. 10:37). The unbelieving world and the unbelief of your own heart may say, as those atheistic scoffers do, "Where is the promise of his coming? Do not all things continue as they were from the beginning of the creation?" But let us be sure that the Lord is not slack concerning his promises, as some men count slackness. One day is with him like a thousand years, and a thousand years like one day (2 Pet. 3:4, 8–9).

I thought on this many times when I was with the army approaching the towns and castles of the enemy. With what glad hearts all the poor prisoners within heard the news and beheld our approach. How they ran up to their prison windows and from there beheld us with joy. How glad they were to hear the roar of the same cannon that was the enemy's terror. How they clapped each other on the back and cried, "Deliverance! Deliverance!" And those who had been their insulting, scorning, cruel enemies began to speak to them in fair words and beg their favor. But they did so in vain, for they were not at the disposal of the prisoners but of the general. In the same way, when the conquering Lion of the tribe of Judah will appear with all the hosts of heaven (Rev. 5:5), when he will surprise the careless world as a thief in the night (1 Thess. 5:2), when as the lightning that appears in the east and shines even to the west, so they will behold him coming (Matt. 24:27).

Our Resurrection

The second stream that leads to paradise is that great work of Jesus Christ in raising our bodies from the dust and uniting them again with our soul. Just as we wake up in the morning when we have slept through the night, so will we surely then awake. What does it matter if in death our bodies must become loathsome lumps cast out of the sight of men as not fit to be endured among the living? What if our carcasses become as vile as those of the beasts that perish? What if our bones are dug up and scattered, and worms consume our flesh? Even so, we know that our Redeemer lives, that he will stand on the earth at the last, and that we will see him with our own eyes (Job 19:25–26). Anyway, what is this piece of flesh that you are loath should come to so base a state? It is only the flesh that will suffer all this, the same flesh that has been a clog to our souls for so long.

Remember this: when the earthly house of your tabernacle is dissolved, you will have a building from God, "a house not made with hands, eternal in the heavens" (2 Cor. 5:1). How willingly our soldiers burnt their huts when the siege was ended, being glad that their work was done, that they could go home and dwell in their houses! In a similar way, cheerfully lay down this bag of loathsome filth, this lump of corruption; you will undoubtedly receive it again imperishable and immortal (1 Cor. 15:53). Freely lay down this earthly, natural body;

believe it, you will receive it again as a celestial, spiritual body. Though you lay it down in the dirt with great dishonor, you will receive it in glory and with honor. Though you are separated from it through weakness, it will be raised again and joined to you in mighty power. When the trumpet of God will sound the call, "Come away, arise you dead," who then will stay behind? Who can resist the powerful command of our Lord? When he will call to the earth and sea, "Oh earth, give up your dead; oh sea, give up your dead" (cf. Rev. 20:13), then our Samson will break the bonds of death for us (Judg. 15:13–14).

Paul has told us by the word of the Lord that those who are alive and remain at the coming of the Lord will not precede those who are asleep. For the Lord himself will descend from heaven with a shout, with the voice of the archangel, with the trumpet of God, and the dead in Christ will rise first. Then those who are alive and remain will be caught up together with them in the clouds to meet the Lord in the air, and so we will be forever with the Lord. Oh Christians, comfort one another with these words (1 Thess. 4:15–18). This is one of the gospel mysteries:

> In a moment, in the twinkling of an eye, at the last trumpet: for the trumpet will sound, and the dead will be raised incorruptible, and we will be changed. For this corruptible must put on incorruption, and this mortal must put on immortality. . . . Death is swallowed up in victory. Oh death, where is your sting? Oh grave, where is your victory? . . . Thanks be to God, who gives us the victory through our Lord Jesus Christ. (1 Cor. 15:52–57)

Triumph now, oh Christian, in these promises, for you will shortly triumph in their fulfillment. This is the day that the Lord will make;

we will be glad and rejoice in it (Ps. 118:24). The grave could not keep our Lord, and it cannot keep us. He rose again for us, and by the same power he will cause us to rise. Oh, write those sweet words on your heart: "Because I live, you will live also" (John 14:19). As surely as Christ lives, we will live, and as surely as he is risen, we will rise. We have a life that is hidden with Christ in God, and when Christ, who is our life, appears, then we also will appear with him in glory (Col. 3:3–4). Oh, let us not be like the blinded world that cannot see far off. Let us never look at the grave except to see our resurrection beyond it. Faith is quick sighted and can see as far as that, yes, even as far as eternity. Therefore, let our hearts be glad and our glory rejoice, and our flesh also will rest in hope—for he will not leave us in the grave, nor suffer us then to see corruption (Ps. 16:10).

Our Judgment

The third part of this prologue to the saints' everlasting rest is the public and solemn process of their judgment, where they will first be acquitted and justified, and then with Christ they will judge the world. I call it public, for all the world must appear at the judgment. Young and old of all conditions and nations that ever were from the creation to that day must come now to receive their doom (Rom. 2:16). The judgment will be set, the books opened, and the book of life produced. The dead will be judged according to their works as written in the books, and anyone whose name is not found written in the book of life will be cast into the lake of fire (Rev. 20:12, 15).

Oh terrible, oh joyful day! It will be terrible to those who have let their lamps go out and have not watched but have forgotten the coming of their Lord (Matt. 25:1–13). But it will be joyful to the saints who waited and hoped to see this day! Then the world will behold the goodness and severity of the Lord (Rom. 11:22): on those who perish, severity, but to his chosen ones, goodness. This is when everyone must give an account of his stewardship: every talent of time, health, intelligence, mercies, afflictions, means, and warnings must be accounted for (Matt. 25:14–30; Luke 16:1–13). This is when the sins of youth, sins forgotten, and secret sins will all be laid open before angels and men. Those who are judged will see all their friends, their wealth, their old delights, all their confidence and false hopes of heaven forsake them. They will see the Lord Jesus whom they neglected, whose word they disobeyed, whose ministers they abused, and whose servants they hated, now sitting to judge them. Their own consciences will cry out against them and call to remembrance all their misdoings.

But why should you tremble, oh humble, gracious soul? Have I made sad the soul that God would not have sad? Does your Lord not know his own sheep who have heard his voice and followed him (John 10:3–4, 14, 27)? Oh then, let the heavens rejoice, the sea, the earth, the floods, and the hills, for the Lord comes to judge the earth (Ps. 96:11–14). With righteousness he will judge the world, and the people with equity (Ps. 98:9). Let Mount Zion hear and be glad, and her children rejoice (Ps. 48:11). For when God rises in judgment, it is to save the humble of the earth (Ps. 76:9). They have judged and condemned themselves during many a day of heartbreaking confession, and therefore they will not be judged to condemnation by the Lord. For there is no condemnation for those who are in Christ Jesus, who do not walk after the flesh but after the Spirit (Rom. 8:1, 4).

Who will bring any charge against God's elect (Rom. 8:33)? Will the law condemn us? No! Whatever the law says, it says to those who are under the law. But we are not under the law but under grace, for the law of the Spirit of life, which is in Christ Jesus, has made us free from the law of sin and death (Rom. 6:14; 8:2). Will conscience condemn us? No! We were long ago justified by faith and so have peace with God (Rom. 5:1). Our hearts have been sprinkled from an evil conscience (Heb. 10:22). The Spirit bears witness with our spirits that we are the children of God. It is God who justifies; who will condemn (Rom. 8:16, 33–34)? If our Judge does not condemn us, who will?

Oh, what inexpressible joy this brings the believer. Our dear Lord who loves our souls and whom our souls love will be our Judge. Will a man fear to be judged by his dearest friend or his brother or father? Will a wife fear to be judged by her own husband? Christ came down to suffer, weep, bleed, and die for you, and will he now condemn you? He was judged, condemned, and executed in your place, and will he now condemn you himself? It has cost him so dearly to save you, even his own blood, and will he now destroy you? He has done most of the work already, in redeeming, regenerating, sanctifying, justifying, preserving, and perfecting you, and will he undo all that at the end? No!

Though Satan accuse us, we have our answer at hand, and our guarantor has discharged our debt. Our Lord will answer for us himself: "They are mine and will be counted my treasured possession. For their transgressions I was struck down and cut off from the land of the living. For them I was bruised and put to grief. My soul was made an offering for their sin, and I bore their transgressions. I have healed them by my stripes; I have justified them by my knowledge. They are my sheep, and who will take them out of my hands?" (cf. Isa. 53:4–5, 8, 11; Mal. 3:17; John 10:28). This is the glorious day of the believers' full justification.

Our Coronation

The fourth and highest step to the saints' advancement is their solemn coronation and reception into the kingdom. The crown of righteousness, which was laid up for them, will be given to them on that day by the Lord, the righteous Judge (2 Tim. 4:8). Those who have been faithful unto death will receive the crown of life (Rev. 2:10). According to the improvement of their talents here, so will their rule and dignity be enlarged. The Lord himself will give them possession with these applauding expressions: "Well done, good and faithful servant. You have been faithful over a few things; I will make you ruler over many things. Enter into the joy of your Lord" (Matt. 25:21, 23). For Christ will take them and sit them with himself on his own throne and will give them power over the nations, even as he received power and authority from his Father. He will give them the morning star (Rev. 2:26–28). With this solemn and blessed proclamation will he enthrone them: "Come, all you who are blessed of my Father, and inherit the kingdom prepared for you from the foundation of the world" (Matt. 25:34). This is the holding forth of the golden scepter, to allow our approach into the glory of the King (Est. 5:2). Come now as near as you like, for the enmity is utterly taken away.

And thus we have by the plumb line of Scripture fathomed this fourfold stream, and we have seen the Christian safely landed in paradise. This four-wheeled, fiery chariot has carried the saint honorably to his rest (2 Kings 2:11–12; Ezek. 1:15–21). Now let us view those mansions and consider his privileges a little further and see whether there be any glory like the saint's glory.

Questions for Reflection

1. To what extent do you live in the confident expectation of Christ's return? Do you share Baxter's excitement and anticipation?

2. Do you think much on your own death? What emotions does it stir within you when you do?

3. How does Baxter's description of the saints' entrance into heaven inspire and encourage you?

4. How might it change your way of life if you kept this heavenly prospect firmly in view?

The Excellent Properties of This Rest

Having considered the saints' entrance into heaven, Baxter returns to reflect on the nature of their everlasting rest. He identifies eight qualities that characterize this rest. He marvels at what our experience will be: so different from our earthly predicament, so utterly above what our merits deserve, and so lovingly, freely, and graciously given by God through the work of Christ.

—

THE NEXT THINGS I will handle are the excellent properties of this rest. They will adorn the crown of the saints like so many jewels.

Our Rest Is Both Costly and Free

The first quality of our rest is that it is costly. It has been purchased at a price (1 Cor. 6:20), even the blood of the Son of God (Acts 20:28). There is no greater love than to lay down one's life (John 15:13). Surely, then, love is the most precious fragrance in the whole garland, and of all the flowers that grow in the garden of love, is there one more sweet and beautiful than this blood? Oh, how will it fill our souls to have our Redeemer forever before our eyes and to have the liveliest sense and freshest remembrance of that dying, bleeding love always upon us. Now we are dulled with vile, senseless hearts. We can hear and read about all the sufferings of his life-giving love and still be unmoved and unaffected. But then our perfected souls will feel as well as hear. With feeling apprehensions they will flame again in love for love. When the obstructions between the eye and the understanding are taken away, and the passage opened between the head and the heart, surely our eyes will everlastingly affect our heart. As we view with one eye our slain-revived Lord and with the other eye our lost-recovered souls and our transcendent glory, these views will eternally pierce us and warm our very souls. We will leave these hearts of stone and rock behind us and the sin that clings so closely (Heb. 12:1), and we will behold, as it were, the wounds of love with the eyes and hearts of love forever.

The second pearl in the saints' crown is that our rest is free. These two attributes, purchased and free, are the two chains of gold that make up that wreath for the heads of the pillars in the temple of God (1 Kings 7:17). Our salvation was costly to Christ but free to us. Oh, the everlasting admiration that must seize the saints to think of this freeness! What did the Lord see in me that he should judge me fit for such a state? That I, who was but a poor, diseased, despised wretch, should be clad in the brightness of this glory? That I, who was so recently groaning, weeping, dying, should now be as full of joy as my heart can hold? That I should be taken from the grave, where I was rotting and stinking, and from the dust and darkness, where I seemed forgotten, and now here be set before his throne? Oh, who can fathom immeasurable love!

Ah, Christian, there is no talk of our worthiness or unworthiness. If worthiness were our condition for admission, we would sit down with

John and weep because no one in heaven or earth is found worthy. But the Lion of the tribe of Judah is worthy, he has prevailed (Rev. 5:3–5), and by that title must we hold the inheritance. What an astonishing thought it will be, to think of the immeasurable difference between what we deserve and what we receive, to look down on those in hell and see the vast difference that free grace has made between us and them, and to see the inheritance there that we were born to, so different from that which we have been adopted to! That death was the wages of my sin, but this eternal life is the gift of God through Jesus Christ my Lord (Rom. 6:23).

We know to whom the praise is due. Indeed, it was to this very end that infinite wisdom cast the whole design of man's salvation into this mold of purchase and freeness, so that the love and joy of man might be perfected and the honor of grace most highly advanced. The thought of merit will neither cloud the one nor obstruct the other, and on these two hinges the gates of heaven will turn. So then, let *Deserved* be written on the door of hell, but on the door of heaven and life itself, *The Free Gift*.

Our Rest Is Corporate and Immediate

The third attribute of this rest is that it is in the fellowship of all the blessed saints. The strings of a musical instrument do not receive their sound and sweetness from each other, yet their concurrence causes a harmony that could never be produced by one string alone. For those who have prayed, fasted, wept, watched, and waited together, now their pleasure will only be advanced to joy and praise together.

I am convinced of this, fellow Christians: As we have been together in the labor, duty, danger, and distress, so will we be together in the great recompense and deliverance. As we have been scorned and despised together, so will we be crowned and honored together. As we have gone through the day of sadness together, so will we enjoy together that day of gladness. Those who have been with us in persecution and prison will be with us also in that palace of consolation. All our praises will make up one melody, all our churches one church, and all ourselves but one body—for we will be one in Christ, even as he and the Father are one (John 17:21).

To think of such a friend who died at such a time, such a precious Christian slain at such a battle, and another saint killed at another fight (oh, what a number of them I could name)—and that all of them have entered into rest. They will not return to us, but we will surely go to them. Some people ask if we will know each other in heaven. Surely no knowledge will cease except that which implies our imperfection, and what imperfection can this imply? No, our present knowledge will be increased beyond belief. It will indeed be put away but only as the light of the candle and stars is put away by the rising of the sun, which is more a putting away of our ignorance than of our knowledge. Indeed, we will not know each other in the way we do now: not by stature, voice, color, face, complexion, or outward shape; not by gifts of learning, by titles of honor and worldly dignity, by youth or age, or, I think, by sex. Instead, we will know and be known by the image of Christ, by spiritual relation, and by former faithfulness in improving our talents. It is not only our old acquaintances whom we will know and enjoy but all the saints of all the ages, whose faces in the flesh we never saw.

Another excellent property of our rest is that we will receive the joys of our rest immediately from God. The truth is, even the best of men apprehend only a little of what God expresses in his word, and what they apprehend they are unable to put into words. Through our own unbelief, stupidity, laziness, and other corruptions, we usually fail in what we might declare, and the darkness of our people's understandings and the sad senselessness of their hearts usually shut out and make void even the little that we can declare. As all the works of God are perfect in their season, just as he is perfect, so all the works of man in himself are imperfect. Those works that God performs by the hand of man will too much savor of the instrument. The comforts that flow through sermons, sacraments, reading, company, conversation, and creatures are but half comforts, and the life that comes by all these is only a half-life in comparison to those the Almighty will speak with his own mouth.

While we may find joy in what we receive from a distance, the fullness is in God's own presence. Oh Christian, you will then know the difference between the creature and the Creator—and the contentment that each of them affords. We will then have light without a candle and a perpetual day without the sun. For the city has no need of the sun or the moon to shine in it, for the glory of God and the Lamb is its light (Rev. 21:23; 22:5). We will then have communion without sacraments, when Christ will drink with us of the fruit of the vine anew (Matt. 26:29). That is, he will refresh us with the comforting wine of immediate enjoyment in the kingdom of his Father. To have needs but no supply is the case of those in hell; to have needs supplied by the means of creatures is the case of us on earth; to have needs supplied immediately from God is the case of the saints in heaven; to have no needs at all is the prerogative of God himself. The more of God we see and receive by the means of the creature here, the nearer our state will be to what we will enjoy in glory. We will live in our Father's house and presence. God will be all and in all (1 Cor. 15:28). Then we will indeed be at home in rest.

Our Rest Is Seasonable and Suitable

A fifth attribute of our rest is that it is seasonable. If God expects the fruit of his vineyard in season (Mark 12:2; Luke 20:10), and if he makes his people as trees planted by the waters, fruitful in their season (Ps. 1:3), he will also give them their crown in season. If he will have the words of joy spoken to the weary in season (Isa. 50:4), he will surely cause that time of joy to appear in the fittest season. If God has appointed the weeks of the harvest in its season, and if he has by an unbreakable covenant established day and night in their seasons, then surely the harvest of the saints and their day of gladness will not miss its season.

When we have completed a long and tedious journey through no small dangers, is home not then seasonable? When we have had a long and perilous war, been forced to maintain a perpetual watch, lived in the midst of furious enemies, and received from them many a wound, would a peace with victory not now be seasonable? Where can you go where the voice of complaining does not show that men live in a continual weariness? Many complain under the pressures of the times: they are weary of their taxes, of plundering, of fear and danger, of poverty and lack. And is rest not seasonable? Some of us are languishing under continual weakness and groaning under most grievous pains. We cry out in the morning, "If only it were evening!" and in the evening, "If only it were morning!" We are weary of going, of sitting, of standing, of lying, of eating, of speaking, of waking, of our very friends, and yes, weary of our very selves. Oh, how often has this been my own case. And is rest not seasonable?

That is especially true of the saints. Listen to any of their conversations, and you will hear by their moans what it is that ails them. Some are weary of a blind mind with its doubts concerning the way they walk; they are unsettled in almost all their thoughts. Some are weary of a hard heart, some of a proud heart, some of a passionate heart, and some are weary of all of these. Some are weary of their daily doubts and fears concerning their spiritual condition. Some are weary of the absence of spiritual joy, and some of the sense of God's wrath. And will rest not then be seasonable for all of these? When a poor Christian has desired, prayed, and waited for deliverance many a year, is it not then seasonable? When he is ready almost to give up and say, "I am afraid I will not reach the end and that my faith and patience will scarcely hold out," is that not a fit season for rest?

A further excellent property of this rest is that it is suitable to the natures, desires, and necessities of the saints.

1. This rest is suitable to their natures. The choicest dishes we enjoy would be to an animal an unpleasing, insufficient sustenance. Even among men, you know the proverb: one man's meat is another man's poison. But suitability and excellency meet in our everlasting rest. Neither gold and earthly glory nor temporal crowns and kingdoms could make a rest for saints. As they were not redeemed at so low a price, so they are not endowed with so low a nature (1 Pet. 1:18, 23). As God will have from them a spiritual worship, suitable to his own spiritual being, so will he provide them with a spiritual rest, suitable to his people's spiritual nature.

Then, dear friends, we will live in our proper element. We are now like a fish in some small container with enough water only to keep it alive, but what is that compared to the full ocean? We have a little air let in to allow us to breathe, but what is that to the sweet and fresh gales on Mount Zion? To be locked up in gold and in pearl would be but a wealthy starving. To have our tables adorned with richly furnished plates and ornaments but no food is only to be richly famished. To be given the sovereignty of all the earth would be only to wear a crown of thorns. To be filled with the knowledge of arts and sciences would be only to further the conviction of our unhappiness. But to have a nature like God and his very image, holy as he is holy, and to have God himself to be our happiness, how well do these things agree?

2. This rest is suitable to the desires of the saints. Here they have a mixed nature. As they are flesh, they have the desires of flesh. As these are not the desires that this rest is suited to, so these desires will not accompany them to their rest. Christian, this rest contains all that your heart can wish for; that which you now long for, pray for, labor for, there you will find it all. Would you rather have God in Christ than all the world? Well, there you will have him. Oh, that we would be wise enough to limit those desires that we know will not be satisfied and to keep up continually in heat and life those desires that will surely have their full satisfaction.

3. This rest is very suitable to the saints' necessities. It contains what they truly lacked. It will not supply them with the lower, created comforts they are now forced to use. These are like Saul's armor on David: more of a burden than a benefit (1 Sam. 17:38–39). But there they will have the benefit without the burden. It was Christ and perfect holiness that they most needed, and with these they will be supplied.

Our Rest Is Perfect and Eternal

The seventh excellency of our rest is that it will be absolutely perfect and complete. We will then have joy without sorrow, rest without weariness. As there will be no mixture of our corruption with our capacities, so we will have no mixture of suffering with our comfort. There will be none of those waves in that harbor that now so toss us up and down. One moment we are at the gates of heaven; in the next we are almost as low as hell. We wonder at those changes of providence toward us, being scarcely two days together in the same condition. Today we are well, and we conclude that the bitterness of death is past; tomorrow we are sick and conclude that we will shortly perish by our illness. Today we are in esteem, tomorrow in disgrace; today we have friends, tomorrow none; today we are in gladness, tomorrow in sadness. But there is none of this inconstancy in heaven. If perfect love casts out fear (1 John 4:18), then perfect joy must cast out sorrow, and perfect happiness will exclude all the remnants of our misery.

The eighth and last jewel in our crown is that it is an eternal rest. The very prospect of leaving it would otherwise add bitterness to all our joys. In fact, it would pierce us more because of the excellent attributes we would have to forsake. How can we take delight in anything when we know how short that delight will be? While we are servants, we hold what we have only by lease, and that merely for the term of a transitory life. But the son abides in the house forever (John 8:35). Our first and earthly paradise in Eden had a way out but no way back in that we could find; this eternal paradise has a way in but no way out again. It is the saints' everlasting rest.

———

Questions for Reflection

1. Which of these eight qualities of rest do you find most moving? Why?

2. Clearly, Baxter felt a weariness with his world, so profoundly marred by civil war and ill health. Are you weary of the world? Do you long for rest?

3. "Our salvation was costly to Christ but free to us" (p. 54). How might you settle your mind each day in gratitude for what Christ has done?

4. Baxter has presented a picture of the full fruition of what Christ has done and the many blessings that will be ours forever as a result of his work. How might you focus your mind each day on the magnitude of those blessings?

What We Will Rest From

Those who enter into heaven through that four-cornered portico will find
a perfect rest from sin and suffering. Here Baxter celebrates that future
freedom from sin, and he reflects on ten different forms of suffering that
will never again intrude on our happiness, our delight, our joy in God.
Once again, he draws a stark contrast between our lamentable earthly
condition and the blessed nature of our rest to come.

———

THE SAINTS' EVERLASTING REST will comprise both the perfecting of
all our capacities and the complete removal of all our evils. Though that
first, positive part is the sweetest and that which draws the other after it,
just as the rising of the sun excludes the darkness, yet that negative part
is not to be slighted. It will bring our freedom from so many and so great
calamities. Therefore, let us carefully look over these positive freedoms
individually and observe what we will rest from. In general, it is a rest
from all evil: first, from the evil of sin; second, from the evil of suffering.

Rest from Sin

Our rest excludes nothing more directly than sin. Nothing enters heaven
that defiles or does what is detestable or false (Rev. 21:27); when they

are there, the saints are saints indeed. He who has undertaken to present them to his Father without spot or wrinkle but perfectly holy and without blemish (Eph. 5:27; Jude 1:24) will now most certainly perform his undertaking.

Therefore, Christian, never fear this: once you are in heaven, you will sin no more. Is this not glad news to you who have prayed, watched, and labored against sin for so long? I know if you had the choice, you would choose to be freed from sin rather than be made heir of all the world. Well, wait until then, and you will have your desire. That hard heart, those vile thoughts that lie down and rise with you, that accompany you to every duty, that you could no more leave behind than leave your very self behind, will now be left behind forever. They might accompany you to death, but they cannot proceed a step further.

Have no doubt, we will no longer retain this rebelling principle that is constantly withdrawing us from God and addicting us to backsliding. We will no more be oppressed with the power of our corruptions or vexed with their presence. No pride, passion, slothfulness, or senselessness will enter with us; no strangeness to God and to the things of God; no coldness of affections or imperfection in our love; no uneven walking or grieving of the Spirit; no scandalous action or unholy walking. We will rest from all these forever.

Rest from Suffering

Our rest will also be a perfect rest from suffering. When the cause is gone, the effect ceases. Our sufferings were the consequences of our sinning, and they will both cease together. I will show ten particular kinds of suffering from which we will rest.

1. We will rest from all our perplexing doubts and fears. It will no more be said that doubts are like the thistle, a bad weed growing in

good ground. They will be weeded out and trouble the gracious soul no more. The full fruition of love itself has now resolved our doubts forever. We will hear this kind of language no more: "How will I know that God is my Father, that my heart is upright, that my conversion is true, that my faith is sincere? Oh, I am afraid that my sins are unpardoned. I fear that all I do is only in hypocrisy. I fear that God will reject me from his presence. I doubt he hears my prayers, for how can he accept so vile a wretch, so hard-hearted a sinner as I am?" All this kind of language will be turned into another tune, even into the praises of him who has forgiven, who has converted, who has accepted, yes, who has glorified a wretch so unworthy. It will be as impossible to doubt and fear as it is now to doubt the food in our bellies or to fear that it is night when we see the sun shining.

2. We will rest from all that sense of God's displeasure, which was our greatest torment. For he will cause his fury toward us to rest and his jealousy to cease; he will be angry with us no more (Ezek. 16:42). Hell will surely not be mixed with heaven. Hell is the place for the glorifying of justice, prepared for the purpose of manifesting God's wrath, but heaven is only for mercy and love.

3. We will rest from all the temptations of Satan with which he continually disturbs our peace. What a grief it is to a Christian to be tempted to play with the baits of sin and sometimes to venture on the delights of flesh and even to flat atheism itself. We know the treachery of our own hearts: they are like tinder or gunpowder, ready to catch fire as soon as a spark falls on them. Oh, how the poor Christian lives in continual disquiet who feels these motions, who despairs that his heart should be the soil for this seed and the too-fruitful mother of such an offspring. But here is our comfort: when the day of our deliverance comes, we will fully rest from these temptations. Satan is then bound

up, the time of tempting is done, and the victorious saints will have triumph in place of temptation. Now we walk among his snares and are in danger of being surrounded by Satan's methods and wiles, but then we will be entirely above his snares and out of the hearing of his enticing charms. He has power to tempt us here in the wilderness, but he will not enter the holy city.

4. We will rest not only from the temptations of Satan but also from those of the world and the flesh. Oh, the hourly dangers that we poor sinners walk in! Every part of our body is a snare, every creature is a snare, every mercy is a snare, and every duty is a snare to us. We can barely open our eyes and we are in danger. If we think about those above us, we are in danger of envy; if we consider those below us, we are in danger of contempt. If we see sumptuous buildings, pleasant habitations, honor, and riches, we are in danger of being drawn away with covetous desires; if we see the rags and beggary of others, we are in danger of self-applauding thoughts and an unkind lack of mercy. If we see beauty, it is a bait to lust; if we see deformity, it draws us to loathing and disdain. But blessed be omnipotent love that saves us out of all these temptations. Now our houses, clothes, sleep, food, medicine, father, mother, wife, children, friends, goods, and lands are all so many temptations, and we ourselves are the greatest snare to ourselves. But in heaven the danger and trouble are over.

5. As we rest from all temptations, so we will rest from all abuse and persecution that we suffer at the hands of wicked men. We will be scorned, derided, imprisoned, banished, and butchered by them no more; the prayers of the souls under the altar will then be answered, and God will avenge their blood on those who still dwell on the earth (Rev. 6:9–10). Now is the time for crowning with thorns; then is the time for crowning with glory. Dear Christian, consider, in heaven you

will have no discouraging company but only those who will further your work and gladly join heart and voice with you in your everlasting joy and praises. Until then, possess your souls in patience; bind all reproaches as a crown to your heads and esteem them greater riches than all the world's treasures.

6. We will then rest from all our sad divisions and un-Christian quarrels with one another. Even those who here clashed in discord will all come together in blessed concord and make up one melodious choir. Oh sweet, oh happy day, when we will have one judgment, one heart, one church, one common work forever, when Christ is all and in all (Col. 3:11).

7. We will then rest from all that sadness we now experience when we see our brethren in their calamities. Now we may enter many a poor Christian's cottage and see their children ragged, their purse empty, their cupboard bare, their belly empty, and poverty possessing and filling all. How much better will that day be when we will see them filled with Christ, clothed with glory, and lifted up with the richest and greatest princes!

The church on earth is like a hospital in which some groan under a dark understanding and some under a senseless heart. Some groan under various pains and infirmities. Some bewail a whole catalogue of calamities, especially in days of common suffering when nothing appears to our sight but ruin: families ruined, congregations ruined, sumptuous structures ruined, cities ruined, country ruined, court ruined, and kingdoms ruined. Who does not weep when all these bleed? But our day of rest will free us from all this.

Oh, the sad and heart-piercing spectacles that my eyes have seen in four years of civil war: in this fight a dear friend falls down by me; from another battle a precious Christian is brought home wounded or dead; scarcely a month, hardly a week without the sight or noise of war. Surely there is none of this in heaven. Our eyes will then be filled no more, nor our hearts pierced, with such sights of battle. My eyes will never more behold the earth covered with the carcasses of the slain. Our mourning attire will then be turned into the white robes and the garments of gladness (Rev. 3:5).

8. We will rest also from all our own personal sufferings. Oh, the dying life that we now live, as full of sufferings as of days and hours! We are the carcasses that all calamities prey upon. As all our physical senses are the inlets of sin, so they become the inlets of our sorrow. Grief creeps in at our eyes, at our ears, and almost everywhere. Fears devour us and darken our delights, as the frosts nip the tender buds. Cares consume us and feed on our spirits, as the scorching sun withers the delicate flowers. What tender pieces are these dusty bodies? What brittle glasses do we carry about us, how many thousand dangers do they hurry through, and how hard they are to cure once they are cracked? Oh, the multitudes of slender veins, of tender membranes, nerves, fibers, muscles, arteries—and all of them subject to obstructions, tensions, contractions, ruptures, or one thing or another to cause their grief! Each part is a fit subject for pain and fit to communicate that pain to the whole body; no part suffers its pain or ruin alone.

The prospect of rest is indeed acceptable to one like myself, who, in the last ten or twelve years, has barely had a whole day free from some pain or discomfort. Oh, the weary nights and days! Oh, the tedious, nauseous medicines! Is it not desirable to rest from all these? There will then be no crying out, "Oh, my head!" "Oh, my stomach!" "Oh, my sides!" or, "Oh, my bowels!" No! Sin and flesh, dust and pain, will all be left behind. What would we not give now for a little ease, much more for a perfect cure? How then should we value that perfect freedom to come?

If we have some few comforts here, they are hardly enough to sweeten our crosses. If we have some short and smiling intermissions, they offer scarcely time enough to catch our breath and prepare our rigging for the next storm. If one wave passes by, another follows. If the night is over and the day arrives, it will soon be night again. But oh, the blessed tranquility of that heavenly region, where there is nothing but sweet, continued peace! Oh, healthful place, where none are sick! Oh, fortunate land, where all are kings! Oh, that most holy place, where all are priests! How free is that state, where no one is servant to another, except to his supreme monarch! For it will come to pass that on that day the Lord will give us rest from our sorrow, our fear, and the hard bondage in which we have served (Isa. 14:3). Hold out a little longer, oh my soul, and bear with the infirmities of your earthly tabernacle, for soon you will rest from all your afflictions.

9. We will also rest from all the trouble and pain of duty. The conscientious officeholder now cries out, "Oh, the burden that lies on me!" The conscientious parents who know the preciousness of their children's souls and the constant care required for their godly education cry out, "Oh, the burden!" The conscientious minister, when he has learned what it is to study, pray, and preach according to the weight and excellency of the work, cries out, "Oh, the burden!" Every conscientious Christian cries out, "Oh, the burden!" or, "Oh, my weakness that makes it so burdensome!" But our rest will ease us of the burden forever.

10. Lastly, we will rest from all those sad feelings that necessarily accompany our absence from God. We will no more look into our cabinet and miss our treasure or look into our hearts and miss our

Christ, but all will be concluded in a most full and blessed enjoyment. But because I touched on this before, I will say no more.

Thus I have endeavored to show you a glimpse of the approaching glory. But my expressions fall too far short of its excellency. Reader, if you are a humble, sincere believer and wait with longing and laboring for this rest, you will shortly see and feel the truth of all this, and then you will have a full apprehension of this blessed state. Let even the little I have said kindle your desires and energize your efforts. Be up and doing; run, strive, fight, and hold on, for you have a certain glorious prize before you (1 Cor. 9:24). What kind of men do you think Christians would be in their lives and duties if they kept this glory fresh in their thoughts? What frame would their spirits be in if their thoughts of heaven were lively and believing? Would their hearts be so heavy and their countenance so sad? Would they look to find their comfort in things here below? Would they be so loath to suffer and so afraid to die? Or would they not think every day a year until they could enjoy their rest? The Lord heal our carnal hearts, lest we do not enter into his rest because of our unbelief (Heb. 3:19).

———

Questions for Reflection

1. Do you discern within you a "rebelling principle that is constantly withdrawing [you] from God and addicting [you] to backsliding" (p. 64)? Take a few moments to contemplate what it will be like for that "rebelling principle" to be gone forever.

2. In general, we live in relatively affluent, comfortable conditions, not civil war and chronic sickness. How do the different conditions of

our current context make it harder to appreciate and contemplate our future rest?

3. Is it possible that Baxter is too pessimistic about our condition here on earth? Might we encounter more joy and comfort here than he allows? Why or why not?

4. Baxter offers a list of ten forms of sufferings that will be utterly removed from our experience of rest. Which of those ten particularly weigh on you right now? How does it feel when you look forward to their removal?

A Multitude of Reasons
to Move You

Baxter writes this book to persuade us to practice regular contemplation of heaven and to pursue a life that will obtain everlasting rest. But he is well aware of how few Christians practice the kind of heavenly life that he is proposing. He has a clear-eyed sense of the impediments we will face and the reluctance we will encounter, especially in our own hearts. So he piles on reason after reason—fifty reasons in just this one chapter—to persuade us and motivate us to the work. Each one is necessarily brief, but we may find them cumulatively compelling.

———

IF THIS REST for the saints is so certain and so glorious, why do we not seek after it more earnestly? One would think that a man who heard of such unspeakable glory to be obtained and who believed what he heard to be true would immediately be moved with the urgent desire to seek after it. He might almost forget to eat or drink. He would think of nothing else and speak of nothing else except how to gain assurance and possession of this treasure. Yet Christians who hear of this rest daily and who profess to believe it without doubt as a fundamental article of their faith do as little mind it, care for it, and labor for it and do as much forget it and disregard it as if they had never heard of any such thing or did not believe one word that they heard.

Any man might wonder when he sees what riding and running, what scrambling and catching there is for things that count for nothing, while eternal rest lies neglected. What contriving and caring, what fighting and battling, all to get a step higher in the world than their brethren, while they neglect the kingly dignity of the saints. What unwearied diligence in raising their children, in enlarging their possessions, in gathering a little silver or gold? In the meantime, their judgment is drawing near. Yet they never go to the trouble of even one hour's sober consideration of how that judgment will go with them. They live as if it were only their work to provide for their bodies and only God's work to provide for their souls.

Alas, what a vast gulf there is between our light and our heat, our profession and prosecution. How still we stand. How idly we work. How we talk, jest, and trifle away our time! I think none of us are in good earnest for our souls. We dally with the work of God and play with Christ like children who toy with their food when they should eat it.

I hope, reader, by this time you realize what a desperate thing it is to trifle about our eternal rest and how deeply you have been guilty of this yourself. I hope that you do not now dare to allow this conviction to die but are resolved on another course for the time to come. What do you say? Is this your resolution? Then fall to work speedily and seriously, and bless God that you still have time to do it. Though the past cannot be recalled, redeem the time now by doubling your diligence. So you can see that I do not urge you to this end without cause, I will offer you a multitude of reasons to move you. Do not take them by number but by weight. Their intent is to drive you from delaying and loitering in seeking rest. The Lord open your heart and fasten his counsel effectually on you.

Thirty Arguments for All to Consider

1. Our affections and actions should be somewhat answerable to the greatness of the ends to which they are intended.

2. Our diligence should be somewhat answerable to the greatness of the work we have to do, as well as to the ends of it.

3. Our diligence should be enlivened by the shortness and uncertainty of the time allotted us for the performing of all this work. Yet a few days, and we will be here no more. Time passes on.

4. Our diligence should be somewhat answerable to the diligence of our enemies in seeking our destruction (1 Pet. 5:8).

5. Our affections and endeavors should bear some proportion with the talents we have received and the means we have enjoyed (Luke 12:48).

6. The vigor of our affections and actions should be somewhat answerable to the great cost bestowed on us and to the deep engaging mercies we have received from God.

7. All the relations in which we stand toward God call for our utmost diligence. Should the pot not be wholly at the service of the potter and the creature at the service of his great Creator? Are we his children, and do we not owe him our most tender affections and dutiful obedience? Are we the spouse of Christ, and do we not owe him our observance and our love?

8. How carefully should they work who are spurred on by the afflictions God sends? Is it not easier to endure the labor than the spur?

What haste should they make who have such rods at their backs? Would we prefer to be afflicted like this than to be up and going?

9. The angels are ministering spirits for the service of the elect (Heb. 1:14). Is it not an intolerable crime for us to trifle while all the angels are employed to assist us?

10. Should our affections and endeavors not be answerable to the acknowledged principles of our Christian profession? The very fundamental doctrines of our religion are that God is the chief good and that all our happiness consists in his love. Therefore, this rest in him should be valued and sought above all things.

11. No man can obey or serve God too much. How eager and faithful should we be in that work where we are sure we can never do enough?

12. It is the nature of every supporting grace to urge the soul on to diligence and speed. If you loved God, you would make haste and not delay or trifle. You would think nothing too much that you could possibly do. You would be ambitious to serve him and please him even more.

13. Those who trifle in the way to heaven will lose all their labor, but serious endeavors will obtain their end. If two men are running in a race, he who runs slowest may as well never have run at all, for he loses both the prize and his labor.

14. We have lost a great deal of precious time already. With some of us, our childhood and youth are gone. With others, their middle age is past. The time before us is very uncertain and short. If it is sure enough that we have lost so much of our lives, let us not now be so foolish as to lose the rest (1 Pet. 4:1–4).

15. The greater your laying out, the greater your comings in. Whatever you do, whatever you suffer, this everlasting rest will pay for all. There will be no repenting of our labors or sufferings in heaven.

16. Laborious striving for salvation is the way that the wisdom of God has directed us to as best and necessary. Who knows the way to heaven better than the God of heaven?

17. There is not a man who ever was or is or will be who will not one day justify the diligence of the saints and approve of their wisdom. Who would not go on in the way that everyone will applaud in the end?

18. Even those who have been the most serious, careful Christians exceedingly lament their negligence when they come to die. They wish that they had been a thousand times more holy, more heavenly, and more laborious for their souls.

19. Consider how far many a man goes and what a deal of care he takes for heaven and yet misses it for lack of more. Not every man who strives will be crowned (2 Tim. 2:5).

20. God has resolved that heaven will not be had on easier terms. He has not only commanded it as a duty but has tied our salvation to the performance of it. Rest can only follow labor.

21. God is in good earnest with you; why then should you not be in good earnest with him? In his commands he means as he speaks, and he will surely require your real obedience.

22. Christ was serious in purchasing our redemption. There was no jesting in this. So should not we be serious in seeking our own salvation?

23. The Holy Spirit is serious in urging us on to our happiness. He strives with our hearts (Gen. 6:3). He is grieved when we resist him (Eph. 4:30). Should we not then be serious in obeying his motions?

24. God is serious in hearing our prayers, delivering us from our dangers, removing our troubles, and bestowing his mercies. Will we be so slight in the work of God when we expect that he should be so regardful of us? Will we receive real mercies and then return such superficial and frothy service?

25. The ministers of Christ are serious in instructing and exhorting you. Why should you not be as serious in obeying their instructions?

26. How serious and diligent are all the creatures in their service to you: the sun, the rivers, the harvests? Will all these be laborious and only you negligent? Will they all be serious in serving you, and yet you be so slight in your service to God?

27. The servants of the world and the devil are serious and diligent. They ply their work continually, as if they could never do enough. Do you not have a better Master, sweeter employment, greater encouragements, and a better reward?

28. There was a time when you were serious yourself in your service to Satan and the flesh, when you were addicted to common ways, evil company, or sinful delights. Will you not now be more earnest and diligent for God?

29. Even now, you are in good earnest about the matters of this life. If you are sick, what serious groans and complaints do you utter? If your pain is great, the whole town will quickly know it. Are you not in a fight for your lives, and is it time to sleep? Are you not in a race, and is there not the prize, the crown of glory (1 Cor. 9:24; 2 Tim. 4:7–8)? Should you then sit still or take your ease?

30. There is no jesting in heaven or in hell. The saints have a real happiness and the damned a real misery. I can see you being astonished as you look back and wonder how you could possibly make light of these things! I hear you crying out at your stupidity and madness!

Ten Questions for Further Conviction

Reader, having laid down these undeniable arguments for you, I here in the name of God demand your resolution. Will you yield obedience or not? I am confident that your conscience is convinced of your duty; dare you now go on in your careless course against the plain evidence of reason, the commands of God, and the light of your own conscience? Because I know the strange obstinacy and rockiness of the heart of man, and because I am determined to drive in this nail to the head, I will proceed with you a little further in these following questions. Do not stifle your conscience or resist conviction, but answer them faithfully and obey accordingly.

1. If you could grow rich by religion or get lands and lordships by being diligent in godliness, what kind of life would you lead? What pains would you take in the service of God? Is the rest of the saints not a more excellent happiness than all this?

2. If the law of the land punished with death every breach of the Sabbath, every omission of family duties or secret duties, or every cold and heartless prayer, what manner of life would you lead? Is eternal death not more terrible than temporal death?

3. If it were God's ordinary course to punish every sin with some present judgment, what kind of life would you lead? Is not eternal wrath more terrible than all this?

4. If one of your old companions in sin came back from the dead to tell you that he suffers the torments of hell for living such a careless, worldly, ungodly life as you now live and to advise you to take another course, how would this take with you? What manner of person would you then be?

5. If you knew that this was the last day you had to live in the world, how would you spend it? If you knew when you went to bed that you would not rise in the morning, would your thoughts of another life not be more serious that night?

6. If you had seen the general dissolution of the world and all the pomp and glory of it consumed to ashes, what would that sight

persuade you to do? Such a sight you will certainly see. "What manner of persons ought you to be in all holy conduct and godliness" (2 Pet. 3:11)?

7. If you had seen the judgment set and the books opened with most trembling on the left hand of the Judge, what manner of person would you be after such a sight as this? You will one day see this sight as surely as you live. Why should that foreknowledge not awaken you to your duty?

8. What if you had seen all the damned in hell in their torments and had heard them wishing that they had another life to live? What a life would you lead after such a sight as this?

9. Imagine you had lain in hell for even one day or hour, and you had felt all those torments that now you only hear about, and then God returned you to the world to see whether you would live any better. What manner of person would you be?

10. Imagine you had experienced just one year of the glory of heaven and there joined with the saints and angels in beholding God and singing his praise, and after that you were returned to the world. What a life would you lead? What pains would you take rather than be deprived of such incomparable glory?

Ten Questions for the Godly

I am sure I have said enough, if not to stir up the lazy sinner to a serious working out of his salvation, yet at least to silence him and leave him inexcusable at the judgment of God. If after reading all this, you can go on in the same neglect of God and your soul and draw out the rest of your life in the same dull and careless course as you have done until now, then I have no more to say to you. I may as well speak to a post or a rock. But I will add a few more words to the godly in particular, to show them why they above all men should be laborious for heaven. To this end, I desire them soberly to answer these ten questions.

1. What manner of persons should they be whom God has chosen to be vessels of mercy (Rom. 9:23) and has given the very cream of his blessings, the special love of the Father, and the promise and seal of everlasting rest? Tell me in good earnest, what kind of lives should they live?

2. What manner of persons should they be who have felt the pain of their negligence as much as the godly have done and are likely enough to feel it again if they do not reform it? Surely they should be so slothful no more.

3. What manner of persons should they be in holy diligence who have been so long convinced of the evil of laziness and have confessed their sin on their knees a hundred and a hundred times, both in public and in private? Should they thus confess their sin and still commit it?

4. What manner of persons should they be in careful godliness who have bound themselves to God by so many covenants as we have done? The Lord pardon our covenant breaking and grant that our own solemn commitments may not condemn us.

5. What manner of persons should they be who are so near to God as we are? We are his children, in his family, still under his eye, the objects of his greatest jealousy as well as his love.

6. What manner of men should they be in duty who have received so much encouragement as we have done by our successes? The sweetness we have tasted in diligent obedience more than outweighs all the pains. Almost all our solid comforts have come by way of close and constant duty. How should we not then above all men ply our work?

7. What manner of men should they be who are still in great uncertainty whether they are sanctified or justified and whether they are the children of God or not, as are most of the godly I meet with?

8. What manner of persons should they be in holiness who have so much of the great work yet undone as we have? We are like a boatman rowing up a river: he can row as hard as he likes for a whole month long, but if he slackens his hand and thinks to ease himself, his boat goes faster down the stream than it went up. It is the same with our souls when we think to ease ourselves by abating our work in duty. Our time is short, our enemies are mighty, our hindrances are many. God seems still at a great distance from many of us. Our thoughts of him are dull, strange, and unbelieving. Our acquaintance and communion with Christ is small, and our desires to be with him are just as small. Should men in our case stand still?

9. What manner of men should they be in their diligence whose lives and duties are so important to the saving or destroying of a multitude of souls? If we slip, many are ready to stumble. If we stumble, many are ready to fall. Therefore, what manner of persons should we be in our duties and examples?

10. What manner of persons should they be on whom the glory of the great God so much depends? Men will judge the Father by the children and the Master by the servants. We bear his image, and therefore men will measure him by his representation. He is nowhere in the world so lively represented as in his saints. Will they set him forth as a patron of viciousness or idleness?

Seeing that all these things are true, I charge you to resolve this final question: What manner of persons ought we to be in all holy conduct and godliness (2 Pet. 3:11)? Let your life answer that question as well as your tongue.

Questions for Reflection

1. Baxter has offered many reasons to live a life that leads to everlasting rest. How persuasive do you find them? Which particular reasons are most compelling?

2. "Rest can only follow labor" (p. 77). Is Baxter right about that? Does the very prospect of heavenly rest imply earthly labor? Why or why not?

3. One of the difficulties Baxter identifies is that we say we believe in heaven and hell but that this belief does not shape our life in an obvious or tangible way. Is that true of you? Do you try to attain both earthly comfort and heavenly rest?

4. If you have been at all compelled by Baxter's reasons, what will you change in the way you live your life?

Why Are We So Reluctant to Die?

Death is a necessary part of our entrance into everlasting rest. Baxter
suspects that our natural reluctance to go through death betrays a
deeper doubt about the rest that lies beyond and a determination to
find our rest now, here on earth, in things below. So he challenges
our expectations of finding rest here on earth, and he questions our
unwillingness to die.

———

"THERE REMAINS THEREFORE a rest for the people of God" (Heb.
4:9). If this rest remains before us, it would be sin and folly to
expect to find it here on earth. Where will we find the Christian
who does not deserve this reproof? Surely we will all cry "Guilty!"
to this accusation. We do not know how to enjoy houses, goods,
lands, and revenues without seeking our rest in these enjoyments.
We seldom, I fear, have such sweet and heart-contenting thoughts
of God and glory as we have of our earthly delights. God usually
has the preeminence in our tongues and professions but not in our
hearts. Do we not desire these earthly enjoyments more devotedly
than we do the Lord himself? If we lose them, does it not trouble
us more than our loss of God? If we lose merely a friend or our

health, all the town will hear of it, but we can miss our God and scarcely bemoan our misery.

This much is obvious: we exceedingly make the creature our rest. Is it not enough that God's mercies and gifts are sweet delights and refreshing helps in our way to heaven? Will we also make them our heaven itself? Christian reader, I would as willingly make you sensible of this sin as of any sin in the world, if I knew how to do it, for the Lord's greatest quarrel with us is in this point. Therefore, I most earnestly beseech you to press upon your own conscience the following considerations.

Correcting Our Expectations of Rest on Earth

1. It is gross idolatry to make any creature or means our rest. We make that creature our god when we settle our soul upon it and say, "Now I am well," simply on the basis of our enjoyment of it.

2. Consider how you contradict the end God intends for these things. He gave them to help you to him; would you take up with them instead? He gave them that they might be comfortable refreshments in your journey; would you now dwell in your inn and go no further? You not only contradict God but lose the benefit that you might receive by these helps and even make them your great hurt and hindrance. Therefore, to rest here is to turn all God's mercies and gifts clean contrary to their own ends and our own advantage and to destroy ourselves with what God intended to help us.

After such an unsettled life and almost five years living in the weary condition of war and the unpleasing life of a soldier, I have myself thought of these enjoyments with too much contentment. I have been too ready to say, "Soul, . . . take your rest" (Luke 12:19). I have comforted myself more in the forethoughts of enjoying these means than I have of coming to heaven and enjoying God. Why should I be surprised, then, if God were to cut me off just as I am sitting down in this supposed rest? Has this not also been your condition? Many of you have been soldiers, driven from house and home, enduring a life of trouble and blood. Did you not reckon up all the comforts you would have when you came back home? Did you not gladden your hearts with such thoughts more than with the thoughts of your coming to heaven? No wonder God now somewhat crosses you and turns some of your joy into sadness. I pray God that you may take warning for the time to come, that you do not rob yourselves of all your mercies.

3. Think of it this way: if God allowed you to take up your rest here, it would be one of the sorest afflictions and greatest curses that could possibly befall you. It would be better for you if you never had a day of ease or contentment in the world, for weariness might then make you seek after your true rest. To have their portion in this life and their good things on the earth is the lot of the most miserable, perishing sinners. So how is it fitting for Christians to expect their rest here? Our rest is our heaven; where we take our rest, there we make our heaven. Would you really have such a heaven as this? Our rest is only in the full obtaining of our ultimate end, but we cannot expect that in this life. Therefore, neither should we expect our rest here on earth.

Should Noah have made the ark his home and have been loath to come forth when the waters subsided (Gen. 8)? Should the sailor make his dwelling on the sea and settle his rest in the midst of rocks and raging tempests? Should a soldier rest in the midst of the fight when he is still in the very thick of his enemies and the instruments of death encompass him? Though he may venture upon war for the obtaining of peace, I hope he is not so mad as to settle for war instead of peace.

And are Christians not like mariners and soldiers? Have we not fears within and troubles without (2 Cor. 7:5)? Are we not in the thick of continual dangers? And will we sit down and rest here? Oh Christian, follow your work, look to your dangers, hold on to the end, win the field, and come off the battleground before you think of a settling rest.

Rejoice in the creature but only insofar as it comes from God, leads to him, or brings you some token of his love. Always remember that even when you have what you desire, this is not heaven but merely the firstfruits. While we are present in the body, we are absent from the Lord (2 Cor. 5:8). While we are absent from the Lord, we are absent from our rest.

Reproving Our Unwillingness to Die

Is there a rest remaining for the people of God? Why then are we so reluctant to die and to depart from here so that we may possess our rest? If I may judge others' hearts by my own, we are exceedingly guilty in this point. We linger, like Lot in the city of Sodom, until God, being merciful, comes to pluck us away against our wills (Gen. 19). Because we are apt to make light of this sin and to plead our common nature, let me here set before you its aggravations and propound some further considerations that may be useful to you and myself against it.

First, consider what gross infidelity lurks in the bowels of this sin: either pagan unbelief of the truth of that eternal blessedness and of the truth of the Scripture that promises it to us, or at least a doubting of our own interest in this rest, or usually somewhat of both of these. Though most Christians feel more deeply their lack of assurance, yet I suspect their doubt of the truth of our rest is the master sin and of greatest force in this business. Oh, if only we truly believed that the promise of this glory is the word of God and that God truly means as he speaks and is fully resolved to make it good; if only we truly believed that there is indeed such blessedness prepared for believers as the Scripture mentions, surely we would be as impatient of living as we are now fearful of dying.

As the weakness of our faith is demonstrated in our unwillingness to die, so also is the coldness of our love. If we love our friend, we love his company. His presence is comfortable; his absence is troublesome. When he goes from us, we desire his return; when he comes to us, we welcome him with gladness; when he dies, we mourn—and usually overmourn. And would these not be our desires after God if we really loved him? If I delight merely in some garden, walk, or gallery, I would often be in it. If I love my books, I often and almost unweariedly read them. The food that I love I often feed on; the clothes that I love I often wear; the recreations that I love I often use; the business that I love I am much employed in. Can I love God above all these and yet have no desires to be with him? Is it not more likely a sign of hatred than of love when the thoughts of our appearing before God are our most grievous thoughts and when we take ourselves as undone because we must die and come to him? I would hardly take him for a true friend who was as content to be absent from me as we usually are to be absent from God.

It appears we are little weary of sinning when we are so unwilling to be freed from sin by dying. If we took sin to be the greatest evil, we would not be willing to remain in its company for so long. If we looked on sin as our cruelest enemy and on a sinful life as the most miserable life, surely we would then be more willing of a change. But oh, how far removed our hearts are from our doctrinal profession! We brand sin with the most odious names that we can imagine, and all far short of expressing its real vileness, but when the approach of death puts us to the trial, we prefer to continue with these abominations rather than enjoy the presence and enjoyment of God.

Oh foolish, sinful heart! Have you not been for long enough a sink of sin, a cage of all unclean lusts, a fountain incessantly streaming forth the bitter and deadly waters of transgression, and are you not yet weary? Have you not yet transgressed in sin, provoked your Lord, or abused his love for long enough? Would you yet grieve the Spirit more, sin against your Savior's blood, increase your own wounds, and still lie under your grievous imperfections? Foolish sinner! Who has wronged you: God or sin? Who has wounded you and caused your groans? Who has made your life so woeful? Is it Christ, or is it your corruption? And are you yet so loath to think of parting from it?

Ah, foolish, wretched soul! Does every prisoner not groan for freedom, every slave desire his jubilee, every sick man long for health, and every hungry man for food, and do you alone abhor deliverance? Does the sailor not long to see the land, does the farmer not desire the harvest, does the laborer not seek his pay, does the traveler not yearn to be at home, does the runner not long to win the prize, does the soldier not desire to win the field? And yet are you loath to see your labors finished, to receive the end of your faith and sufferings, and to obtain the thing for which you live? Are not all your sufferings, griefs, and groans only dreams? If they are, we should not be afraid of waking. The world's delights are mere dreams and shadows. All its glory is like the light of a glowworm or a wandering fire that yields only a tiny light and very little comforting heat in all our doubtful and sorrowful darkness. Or has the world in these its latter days laid aside its ancient enmity? Has it become of late more kind? Has it left behind its thorny, tearing nature? No, we may reconcile ourselves to the world (at our peril), but the world will never reconcile itself to us. Oh foolish, unworthy soul, who would rather wander in this land of darkness, in this barren wilderness, than be at rest with Jesus Christ! If you well knew what heaven is and what earth is, it would not be so.

Consider how we wrong the Lord and his promises, and disgrace his ways in the eyes of the world. It makes the weak ones stagger when they see those who have professed to live by faith and boasted of their hopes in another world so reluctant to lose their hold on present things and go to that glory they talked and boasted about. It confirms worldly sinners in their unbelief and sensuality and makes them conclude, "Surely if these professors really expected so much glory and made so light of the world as they say, they would not themselves be so loath of a change." Oh, how are we ever able to repay the wrong we do to God and poor souls by this scandal? On the other hand, what an honor to God, what a strengthening to believers, what a conviction to unbelievers it would be if Christians answered their professions and cheerfully welcomed the news of their rest.

Our reluctance to depart clearly shows that we have been careless loiterers, that we have spent too much time to little purpose, and that we have neglected a great many warnings. Have we not had all our lifetime to prepare to die, so many years to make ourselves ready for one hour, and are we still so unready and unwilling? Could we have had more frequent warnings? We have seen death raging in towns and fields, so many hundred a day dead of the pestilence, so many thousands slain by the sword, and did we not realize that death would reach to us at last? How many ailments have vexed our bodies? We have passed through frequent languishing, consuming weaknesses, wasting fevers, pain, and trouble—even, it seemed, to the point of death. What were all these but so many messengers sent from God to tell us we must shortly die? They were a lively voice bidding us, "Delay no more, but make ready." And are we still unready and unwilling after all this? Oh careless, dead-hearted sinners, unworthy neglecters of God's warnings, faithless betrayers of our own souls!

The Lord Jesus was willing to come from heaven to earth for us, and will we be unwilling to remove from earth to heaven for ourselves and him? He submitted to a different kind of change from what ours will be. He chose to clothe himself with the garments of flesh, to take on himself the form of a servant (Phil. 2:7), to come from the bosom of the Father's love, and to bear the wrath that we should have borne. He came from heaven down to our hell, from the height of glory to the depth of misery, to bring us up to his eternal rest. Will we really, after all this, be unwilling to die?

Yet do not mistake me in all that I have said. I do not deny that it is lawful and necessary for a Christian to desire God to delay his death for a further opportunity of gaining assurance and also to be serviceable to the church a little longer. But this has little to do with those who are always delaying and never willing, whose true concern is death itself rather than the unseasonableness of dying. Though such desires are sometimes lawful, yet they must be carefully bounded and moderated, which is why I gave the former considerations. The best view is that of Paul's: to be torn between the two, desiring to depart and to be with Christ and yet to remain for as long as God will have us so that we may do the church the utmost service (Phil. 1:23–25). But alas, we are seldom like Paul. Our desires run in only one direction, and that is for the flesh, not the church. Our concern is only the fear of dying.

Questions for Reflection

1. It is only natural to face death with some trepidation. Why does Baxter think we should approach death with something other than fear?

2. Baxter points us to Jesus, who gave up heaven for our hell so that we might have heaven instead of hell. How might Baxter's reminder alter the way we approach both our life and our death?

3. "Our rest is our heaven; where we take our rest, there we make our heaven" (p. 87). Do you agree with Baxter's assertion? To what degree are you subtly trying to cultivate a rest here on earth that can be properly realized only in heaven?

4. How can we prevent ourselves from becoming so comfortable here on earth that we lose the urgency to seek our rest in heaven?

7

The Heavenly Christian Is
the Lively Christian

*For Baxter, regularly focusing our thoughts on heaven is no small
thing. It changes the color and complexion of our whole walk of faith.
If we pursue it diligently, we will gain; if we neglect this duty, we will
lose. A heavenly life is one that makes us joyful, secure, lively, patient,
and profitable. We will honor God, and we will demonstrate that we
really are citizens of another kingdom making our way home.*

———

WE HAVE NOW by the guidance of the word of the Lord and by the
assistance of his Spirit shown you the nature of the saints' everlasting
rest and acquainted you with some duties in relation to it. We will
soon come to the great duty that I chiefly intended when I began this
subject: the regular practice of meditation on that rest. Whoever you
are who reads these lines, I require you, if you offer your allegiance to
the God of heaven and hope for a part in this glory, that you now take
your heart to task. Chide it for its willful strangeness to God. Turn
your thoughts from the pursuit of vanity, bend your soul to study

eternity, busy it about the life to come. Make such contemplations a habitual practice. Do not let those thoughts be seldom and cursory. Settle on them, dwell in them, bathe your soul in heaven's delights, drench your affections in these rivers of pleasure—or rather in this sea of consolation. If your backward soul begins to tire and your loose thoughts start to fly abroad, call them back and hold them to their work. Do not accept their laziness; do not connive at one neglect.

Once you have tried this work, follow it on until you are fully acquainted with it. Keep a close guard on your thoughts until you have some mastery over them. Then you will find yourself in the suburbs of heaven and, as it were, in a new world. You will find that there is indeed sweetness in the work and way of God and that the life of Christianity is a life of joy. You will meet with those abundant consolations for which you have prayed and panted and that so few Christians ever here obtain because they do not know this way or walk in it.

Abundant in Joy and Secure in Temptation

A heavenly mind is a joyful mind. This is the nearest and truest way to live a life of comfort; without this, you must necessarily be uncomfortable. Can a man rest beside a fire and not be warm or sit in the sunshine and not have light? Can your heart be in heaven and not have comfort? When the sun in the spring draws near our part of the earth, see how all things rejoice in its approach. The earth looks green and casts off her bare rags of mourning. The trees shoot forth; the plants revive; the pretty birds, how sweetly they sing. The faces of all things smile on us, and all the creatures rejoice. Beloved friends, if we would just try this life with God and keep our hearts above, what a spring of joy would be within us? How the face of our souls would be changed and all that is within us rejoice. How we would forget our winter sorrows and withdraw our souls from our sad retirements. Oh Christian, get above! Believe it: that region is warmer than this one below.

Must not everything first enter your judgment and consideration before it can delight your heart and affection? God does his work on us as men and in a rational way. He enables and energizes us to consider and study these delightful objects and thus to gather our own comforts as the bee gathers honey from the flowers. Therefore, he who is most skillful and careful in this gathering act is usually the fullest of this spiritual sweetness. Where is the man who can tell me from experience that he has had solid and consistent joy in any other way but this and that God has wrought joy immediately on his affections without the means of his understanding and consideration? It is by believing that we are filled with joy and peace (Rom. 15:13)—and for no longer than we continue our believing. It is in hope that the saints rejoice, even in this hope of the glory of God (Rom. 5:2)—and for no longer than they continue hoping. So then, you may easily see that close meditation on the matter and cause of our joy is God's way to procure solid joy.

Whoever you are, therefore, who reads these lines, I entreat you in the name of the Lord and as you value a life of constant joy to seriously set upon this work and learn this art of heavenly-mindedness. You will gain the increase a hundredfold, and the benefit will abundantly exceed your labor.

Not only will this establish our joy, but a heart in heaven will be a most excellent preservative against temptations. First, it will keep the heart employed. When the mind is either idle or ill employed, the devil does not need a greater advantage. If he finds the mind empty, there is room for anything he wants to bring in. But when he finds the heart in heaven, what hope will he have that any of his motions should take hold? Let him entice us to any forbidden course or show us the bait of any pleasure; the soul will return Nehemiah's answer, "I am doing a great work, so that I cannot come down" (Neh. 6:3). A net or bait that is laid on the ground is unlikely to catch the bird that flies in the air; while she keeps above, she is out of the danger, and the higher she is, the safer she is. So it is with us. Satan's temptations are laid on the earth. How will these ensnare the Christian who has left the earth and walks with God? But alas, we do not stay high for long, but we must return to the earth again, and then we are taken.

Second, a Christian who is consistently conversing above has truer and livelier apprehensions of things concerning God and his soul than any reading or learning can produce. Conversing with wise and learned men is the way to make one wise and learned. So too, he who converses with God becomes wise. If those who travel the earth expect to return home with more experience and wisdom, how much more he who travels to heaven? A dying man is usually wiser than other men, because he looks on eternity as near. He knows he must very shortly be there, so he has deeper and more heart-piercing thoughts of it than ever he could have had in health and prosperity.

Third, while the heart is set on heaven, a man is under God's protection. Therefore, if Satan assaults him, God is more engaged for his defense. He will doubtless stand by him and say, "My grace is sufficient for you" (2 Cor. 12:9). When a man is in the way of God's blessing, he is less in danger of sin's enticing.

Lively, Patient, and Profitable

The diligent keeping of your hearts in heaven will preserve the vigor of all God's work in your soul and put life into all your duties. It is the heavenly Christian who is the lively Christian; it is our strangeness to heaven that makes us so dull. It is the end that gives life to all the means, so the more frequently and clearly we behold this end, the more vigorous we will be. Think how the sailor passes through storms and waves to seek only an uncertain, perishing treasure. Oh, what life would it put into a Christian's endeavors if he were to think often of his everlasting treasure? We run so slowly and strive so lazily because we keep the prize in mind so little.

Therefore, reader, if you lie complaining of deadness and dullness, that you cannot love Christ or rejoice in his love, that you have no life in prayer or any other duty, and yet have never tried this enlivening course, you are the cause of your own complaints. You deaden and dull your own heart. You deny yourself that life you say you desire. Your life is hidden with Christ in God (Col. 3:3). Where must you go for your life except to Christ, and where is he except in heaven? If you lack light and heat, why are you not more in the sunshine? If you would have more of that grace that flows from Christ, why are you not more with Christ? Your strength is in heaven, and your life is in heaven, and every day you must fetch it from there if you are to have it.

The frequent, believing views of glory are also the most precious refreshment in all afflictions. First, they sustain our spirits and soften our sufferings. Second, they keep us from complaining and make us bear our afflictions with patience and joy. Third, they strengthen our resolve not to forsake Christ for fear of trouble. A horse will carry us more cheerfully in travel when he is returning home, where he expects his rest. A man will more quietly endure the lancing of his sores or the cutting out of a kidney stone when he thinks about the relief and ease that will surely follow. What then will a believer not endure when he thinks of the rest to which it tends?

He who has his conversation in heaven is the most profitable Christian to all those about him. When a man is in a strange country and far from home, how glad he is to find one of his own nation. How delightful they find it to talk of their country, of their mutual acquaintances, and of the airs of their home. You may have such a discourse with a heavenly Christian, for he has been there in the Spirit and can tell you of the glory and rest above. If you travel with this man on the way, he will be directing and quickening you in your journey to heaven. If you are buying, selling, or trading with him in the world, he will be counseling you to lay out everything for the inestimable treasure. If you wrong him, he can pardon you, remembering that Christ has not only pardoned greater offenses to him but will also give him this invaluable portion of rest. If you are angry, he is meek, considering the meekness of his heavenly pattern. If he falls out with you, he is quickly reconciled when he remembers that in heaven you must be everlasting friends.

This is the Christian of the right stamp. This is the servant who is like his Lord. And all those about him are the better where they dwell. Oh dear reader, I fear the man I have described is very rare, even among believers, but if it were not for our own shameful negligence, such profitable Christians we all might be. What families, what towns, what nations, what churches should we have, if only they were composed of such Christians. Alas, how empty are the speeches and how unprofitable the society of all other sorts of Christians in comparison to these!

Honoring to God

There is no Christian who so highly honors God as the one who keeps his life in heaven, and without this we deeply dishonor him. It is a disgrace to any father when his children feed on husks, are clothed in rags, and keep company with none but rogues and beggars. Is it not so to our Father when we who call ourselves his children feed on earth, when the clothing of our souls is exactly like that of the naked world, and when our hearts make mere clay and dust their more familiar and frequent company? It is not fitting for the spouse of Christ to live among his kitchen hands and slaves when we can have daily admittance into the chamber of his presence: he holds forth the scepter, if only we will enter (Est. 5:2).

It is just as well we have a Father of tender compassion who will own his children even in dirt and rags and that the Lord knows those who are his (2 Tim. 2:19), or else he would hardly take us for his own, so far do we live below the honor of saints. But oh, how God is honored when a Christian can live above and rejoice his soul in the things unseen. The Lord may say, "Why, this man believes me. I see he can trust me and take me at my word. He rejoices in my promise before he has possession. He can be glad and thankful for that which his bodily eyes have not yet seen. His rejoicing is not in the flesh. I see he loves me, because he trains his mind on me, his heart is with me, he loves my presence, and he will surely enjoy it in my kingdom forever."

The Cost of Neglecting a Heavenly Life

Consider the cost of not diligently keeping your heart in heaven. First, you disobey the flat commands of God. He has made it your duty as well as the means of your comfort. "If you have risen with Christ, seek those things that are above, where Christ sits on the right hand of God. Set your affection on things above, not on things on the earth" (Col. 3:1–2). The same God who has commanded you to believe and to be a Christian has commanded you to set your affections above. The same God who has forbidden you to murder, steal, and commit adultery, incest, or idolatry has forbidden you to neglect this great duty. Dare you willfully disobey him?

Second, you lose the sweetest and most comfortable passages of the word: all those most glorious descriptions of heaven, all those discoveries of our future blessedness, all God's revelations of his purposes toward us, and all his frequent and precious promises of our rest. Are these not the stars in the firmament of the Scripture and the most golden lines in the book of God? Of all the Bible, you should not part with even one of those promises or predictions—no, not for all the world. Yet that is what we do when we neglect this duty.

Third, you frustrate the preparations of Christ for your joy and cause him to speak in vain. All the comforts of the world are worth nothing in comparison to a comforting word from the mouth of God. Will you then neglect and overlook so many of his communications? It has pleased our Father to open his counsel, to let us know the very intent of his heart, to acquaint us with the eternal extent of his love, and he has done all this so that our joy may be full and we might live as the heirs of such a kingdom. Will we now overlook all this, as if he never revealed any such matter? Will we live in earthly cares and sorrows, as if we knew of no such thing? If so, you frustrate the most gracious discoveries of God.

The Appropriateness of a Heavenly Life

It is entirely fitting that our hearts should be set on God when the heart of God is so much set on us. If the Lord of glory can stoop so low as to set his heart on sinful dust, surely one would think we should easily be persuaded to set our hearts on Christ and glory and to ascend to him in our daily affections! Does he not bear you continually in the arms of love, promise that all will work together for your good (Rom. 8:28), suit all his dealings to your greatest advantage, and give his angels to guard you in all your ways (Ps. 91:11)? And will you let your heart cast him by, be taken up with the joys below, and forget your Lord who does not forget you? What ingratitude! Is this not the sin that Isaiah so solemnly calls both heaven and earth to witness against? "The ox knows his owner and the donkey his master's crib. But Israel does not know; my people do not consider" (Isa. 1:3). If the ox or donkey lags behind during the day, it still comes home at night, but we will not so much as even once a day by our serious thoughts ascend to God.

Moreover, our house and home are above (2 Cor. 5:1–2). If you were banished to a strange land, how frequently would your mind return to thoughts of home? How often would you think of your old companions? You would even dream that you were at home, that you saw your father, mother, or friends, and that you were talking with your wife, children, or neighbors. Why is it not like this with us in respect of heaven? Is that not more truly and properly our home, where we must take up our everlasting abode? Here we are strangers; there is our country (Heb. 11:14–15). We are heirs, and that is our inheritance, even an inheritance incorruptible and undefiled that does not fade away, reserved for us in heaven (1 Pet. 1:4). Here we are in continual distress and lack; there lies our substance, even that better and more enduring substance (Heb. 10:34). Here we are beholden to others; there lies our own perpetual treasure (Matt. 6:20–21). Yes, the very hope of our souls is there: all our hope of relief from our distresses; all our hope of happiness, when we are here miserable; all this hope is laid up for us in heaven (Col. 1:5). Why, beloved Christians, do we have so much interest in earth and so few thoughts of heaven? Have we so near a relation and yet so little affection? Are we not ashamed of this?

Lastly, consider that there is nothing else that is worth setting our hearts on. If God does not have our hearts, who or what will have them? What a pity it is that men will not believe God in this until they have lost their labor and heaven and all. What a pity it is that so many Christians who have taken heaven for their resting place lose so many thoughts needlessly on earth and do not care how much they oppress their spirits, which should be kept nimble and free for higher things.

Thus, I have given you these arguments to consider. May they persuade you to a heavenly mind. I now desire you to view them over, read them deliberately, and read them again—then tell me, are they sufficient reason, or are they not? Reader, stop here while you answer my question. Are these considerations weighty or not? Are these arguments convincing or not? Have I proved it your duty and of flat necessity to keep your heart on things above, or have I not? What do you say—yes or no? I know the whole work of man's salvation sticks most at his own will. If we could just get over this block, I see nothing that could stand before us. Be soundly willing, and the work is more than half done. I have next a few plain directions to give you to help you in doing this great work, but alas, it will be in vain to mention them unless you are willing to put them into practice. What say you, reader, are you willing, or are you not? Will you obey if I show you the way of your duty? May the Lord persuade your heart to the work.

———

Questions for Reflection

1. Do you agree with Baxter that keeping our hearts in heaven will make us more effective, authentic, and lively Christians? Why or why not?

2. Are you one of Baxter's readers who complain of "deadness and dullness, that you cannot love Christ or rejoice in his love, that you have no life in prayer or any other duty" (p. 99)? How might the practice of daily meditation on your future rest change your experience?

3. What do you think we will gain by this practice? What will we lose if we neglect it?

4. Baxter has called for an answer—yes or no. Will you resolve to follow his advice or not?

Dangerous Hindrances
and Positive Helps

A heavenly life is hard work and easily frustrated. Here Baxter
works through the main obstacles we will encounter as we seek to
focus regularly on our future rest. He also identifies some aids and
encouragements that will build up our energy and resolve.

———

THE FIRST TASK I must set before you consists in avoiding some
dangerous hindrances that will keep you off from this work, as they
have done for many thousands of souls before you. If I briefly show
you where the rocks lie, I hope you will beware. If I place a sign at
every quicksand, I hope I will need say no more to see you pass safely
by. Therefore, if you value the comforts of a heavenly way of life, I here
charge you on God's behalf carefully to beware of these impediments.

Seven Hindrances to a Heavenly Life

1. The first hindrance is living in a known sin. Oh, what havoc
this will wreak in your soul and the joys that this will destroy! Oh,

the blessed communion with God that this will interrupt and the soul-strengthening duties that this will hinder! Above all others, it is especially an enemy to this great duty of a heavenly life. Christian reader, I desire you in the fear of God to linger here a little and search your heart. Are you one who has abused your conscience with violence? Are you a willful neglecter of known duties? Are you a slave to your appetite, in eating or drinking, or to any other commanding sense? Are you a proud seeker of your own esteem and reputation?

If this is your case, I daresay that heaven and your soul are very great strangers. Surely you are seldom one in heart with God, and there is little hope of change as long as you continue in these transgressions. When you attempt to study eternity and to gather comforts from the life to come, your sin will immediately look you in the face and say, "These things do not belong to you. Why should you take comfort from heaven when you take so much pleasure in the lusts of your flesh?" Oh, how this will dampen your joys and make the thoughts of that day to become your trouble, not your delight. Every willful sin that you live in will be to your comforts as water to the fire: when you think to enliven them, this will quench them; when your heart begins to draw near to God, this will soon come into your mind to cover you with shame and fill you with doubt.

Besides all that, persisting in known sin completely disables you for this work. Your heart is entangled in the lusts of the flesh. It can no more ascend in divine meditation than the bird can fly whose wings are clipped or that is trapped in the snare. Sin cuts the very sinews of the soul; the heavenly life will either make you leave sin, or sin will make you leave the heavenly life—and quickly, for the two cannot continue together.

2. Another hindrance is an earthly mind. You can easily see why this cannot stand with a heavenly mind. God and wealth, earth and heaven, cannot both have the delight of your heart (Matt. 6:24). You will be like a bird with a stone tied to its foot: as soon as you take flight, you will be dragged back to the earth again. Are you one who thinks to be content or happy while still on this earth, who begins to taste sweetness in material gain, who aspires to high standing in the world, who has hatched some thriving projects in your brain, and who is driving on your rising design? Believe it, you are marching with your back toward Christ; you are heading away from this heavenly life. You love to survey your money, your goods, your buildings, or your possessions. Are these not your morning and evening thoughts, while the constant thoughts of a gracious soul will be above with Christ? If he was a fool who said, "Soul, you have enough laid up for many years; take your rest" (Luke 12:19), then what a fool of fools you are, who, knowing this, do not take warning but in your heart speak the same words.

3. A third hindrance is the company of ungodly and sensual men. I am not dissuading you from conversing with them or from showing them love, and especially not from endeavoring the good of their souls for as long as you have opportunity or hope. But alas, our dullness and backwardness are such that we need the most constant and powerful helps. A clod of dirt or a stone that lies on the earth is as likely to arise and fly in the air as our hearts are, in themselves, to move toward heaven. If our spirits do not receive great assistance, they will all too easily be kept from flying aloft even without the least impediment. Therefore, think of this in the choice of your company, and be careful herein.

4. A further hindrance to a heavenly way of life is frequent disputes about lesser truths. I am not persuading you to undervalue the least

truth of God, but let every truth in our thoughts and speeches have their due proportion. Those truths that most closely concern our souls should have an answerable proportion in our thoughts, not heated disputes about lesser truths. He is a rare and precious Christian who is skilled in the improving of well-known truths. Therefore, if you aspire to this joyous life, let me advise you to spend little of your thoughts, time, zeal, or speeches on quarrels that less concern your souls. Then you can feed on the joys above.

5. If you value the comforts of a heavenly life, take heed of a proud and lofty spirit. There is such an antipathy between this sin and God that you will never get your heart near him or get him near your heart as long as this prevails within it. Believe it, dear reader, a proud heart and a heavenly heart are exceedingly contrary. When a man is used to being much with God and taken up in the study of his glorious attributes, he abhors himself in dust and ashes (Job 42:6), and that self-abhorrence is his best preparation to obtain admittance to God again. He will bring them into the wilderness and speak comfortably to them (Hos. 2:14). God delights in a humble soul, who is contrite and who trembles at his word, and the delight of a humble soul is in God; where there is mutual delight, surely there will be the freest admittance, the heartiest welcome, and the most frequent converse (Pss. 34:18; 51:17; Isa. 57:15; 66:2). God resists the proud but gives grace to the humble (1 Pet. 5:5).

Well then, are you someone of worth in your own eyes? Are you overly tender of your esteem in the eyes of others? Do you value people's applause? Do you feel your heart tickled with delight when you hear of your great esteem with men? Are you much dejected when you hear that others slight you? Do you love those best who most highly honor you? Do you serve God only when it contributes to your advancement? Must your judgment be a rule to the judgments of others and your word a law to all about you?

Oh Christian, if you would live continually in the presence of your Lord, lie in the dust, and he will take you up. First descend with him into the grave, and from there you may ascend with him to glory. Learn from him to be meek and lowly, and then you may taste this rest to your soul (Matt. 11:29). Otherwise, your soul will be as the troubled sea that casts about mire and dirt and cannot rest. Instead of these sweet delights in God, your pride will fill you with perpetual disquiet. It is the humble soul who does not forget God, and God will not forget the humble soul (Pss. 9:12; 10:12).

6. Another impediment to this heavenly life is willful laziness of spirit. Truly, I think there is nothing that hinders more than this. If a heavenly life involved only the exercise of the body, the moving of the lips, and the bending of the knee, then it would be an easy work indeed, and men would as commonly step to heaven as they go a few miles to visit a friend. But the work is far more difficult than all this. Reader, heaven is above you and the way is upward, but you are a feeble, short-winded sinner. Do you think to travel daily this steep ascent without a great deal of labor and resolution? If lying down at the foot of the hill and looking toward the top and wishing we were there would serve the turn, then we would have daily travelers to heaven. But "the kingdom of heaven suffers violence, and the violent take it by force" (Matt. 11:12). We must use violence to get these firstfruits as well as to get the full possession. Will your heart move upward without you driving it? Is it not like a dull and jaded horse that will go no longer than he feels the spur?

7. It is also a dangerous and secret hindrance to content ourselves with the mere preparation to this heavenly life while we are utter

strangers to the life itself. We take up with only the study of heavenly things or merely talk about them with one another, as if this were all we needed to make us heavenly people. Oh, that God would reveal to our hearts the danger of this snare. Do not be like one who sits at home to study geography, who draws the most exact descriptions of foreign countries, and yet never sees them or travels toward them. You might describe to others the joys of heaven and yet never come near it in your own hearts. You might fire the hearts of others but never once warm your own hearts.

Ten Helps to a Heavenly Life

Having thus shown you what hindrances will resist you in the work, I will now lay down for you some positive helps.

1. Know heaven to be the only treasure, and labor also to know what a treasure it is. Be convinced that you have no other happiness, and then be convinced what happiness is there. If you do not soundly believe that this is your highest good, you will never set your heart on it. This conviction must sink into your affections, for if it is only a notion, it will have little effect. As long as your judgment undervalues it, your affections will be cold toward it.

2. Labor to know heaven to be the only happiness—and to be your happiness. We can never rejoice in it until we are somewhat persuaded of our title to it. What comfort is it to a naked man to see the rich attire of others or to a man who has not even a morsel to put in his mouth to see a feast he cannot share in? Would all this not rather increase his anguish and make him more sensible of his own misery? Oh Christian, do not rest until you can call this rest your own. Get alone and examine yourself; bring your heart to the bar of trial. If you cannot complete the work well by yourself, seek the help of those who are

skillful. Go to your minister or some able, experienced friend. Open your case faithfully, ask them to deal plainly, and thus continue until you have received assurance. Some doubts may still remain, but you may have sufficient assurance to master them so that they will not much interrupt your peace.

3. Labor to apprehend how near your rest is, and think seriously of its speedy approach. We are more sensible of what we think is near at hand than of what we behold at a distance. When we hear of war or famine in another country, we are not so troubled. But if judgments or mercies begin to draw near, then they affect us. When the plague is in a town twenty miles away, we do not fear it. But if it comes to the next door or if it seizes one of our own family, then we begin to think on it more feelingly. This is true of our mercies as well as our judgments. When they are far off, we talk of them as tales or legends; when they draw close to us, we rejoice in them as truths. This is what makes men think on heaven with so little feeling: they see it at too great a distance. They look on it as twenty, thirty, or forty years away, and this dulls their sense. This expectation of a long life does both the wicked and the godly a great deal of wrong. How much better it is to receive the sentence of death in ourselves and to look on eternity as near at hand (2 Cor. 1:8–10). Surely, reader, you stand at the door, and hundreds of diseases are ready to open the door and let you in. Are not the thirty or forty years of your life that have passed quickly gone? Is it not a very little time when you look back on it? And will not all the rest seem just as fleeting? What a short moment it is between us and our rest. What a small step it is from here into eternity.

4. Another help to this heavenly life is to be talking about it often, especially with those who can speak from their hearts and have

seasoned themselves with a heavenly nature. It is a pity that Christians should ever meet together on earth without some talk of their meeting in heaven. It is a pity so much precious time is spent among Christians in vain discourses, foolish jesting, and useless disputes, with not a sober word of heaven among them. We should meet together to warm our spirits with discussion of our rest. We will say, as the two disciples on the road to Emmaus, "Did not our hearts burn within us . . . while he opened to us the Scriptures?" (Luke 24:32). Get together, then, fellow Christians, and talk of the affairs of your country and kingdom. Comfort one another with such words (1 Thess. 4:18). Should Christians not delight themselves in talking about Christ, and the heirs of heaven in talking of their inheritance?

5. Make it your business in every duty to wind up your affections nearer heaven. What we receive from God is answerable to our own desires and ends. Do not come to your duties with any lower ends. Renounce formality, custom, and applause. When you kneel in secret or public prayer, let it be in hope to get your heart nearer God before you rise. When you open your Bible or other books, let it be with the hope of finding some passage of divine truth and some such blessing of the Spirit with it that may raise your affections nearer heaven and give you a fuller taste of it. When you step out your door on the way to church, say to yourself, "I hope to meet with something from God that may raise my affections before I return. I hope the Spirit will sweeten my heart with celestial delights. I hope that Christ will shine about me with light from heaven, let me hear his instructing and reviving voice, and cause the scales to fall from my eyes, so that I may see more of that glory than I ever saw before (Acts 9:3–4, 18)." If these were our ends and this our course when we set about our duty, we would not be as strange to heaven as we are.

6. Take advantage of every object you see and of everything that happens, so that you may remind your soul of its approaching rest. If you prosper in the world and your labor succeeds, let it make you more aware of your eternal prosperity. If you are weary of your labors, let it make your thoughts of rest more sweet. Is your body refreshed with food or sleep? Remember your inconceivable refreshment with Christ. Do you hear any news that makes you glad? Remember what happy tidings they will be to hear the sound of the trumpet of God and the absolving sentence of Christ our Judge. Are you delighting yourself in the society of the saints? Remember the everlasting, amiable fraternity you will have with perfected saints in their rest. Thus you may see the advantages to a heavenly life that every condition and creature affords us, if only we had the hearts to apprehend and improve them.

7. Be much in that angelic work of praise. The work of praising God, being the most heavenly work, is the most likely to raise us to the most heavenly temper. If we were more taken up in this employment now, we would be more like what we will be then. Little do we know how we wrong ourselves when we exclude from our prayers the praises of God or allow them only a narrow room, while we are copious enough in our confessions and petitions. Reader, I entreat you, let praises have a larger room in your duties. To this end, study the excellence and goodness of the Lord as frequently as your own necessities and vileness. Oh, let God's praise be often in your mouths, for in the mouths of the upright his praise is fitting (Ps. 33:1).

8. Keep your soul with true, believing thoughts of the exceeding, infinite love of God. There can be no doubt that it is the death of our heavenly life to have hard and doubtful thoughts of God, to see him as one who would rather damn us than save us. Oh, if we could always

think of God as we do of a friend, as one who genuinely loves us even more than we do ourselves. If we believed his very heart is set on us to do us good and he has provided for us an everlasting dwelling with himself, it would not be so hard to have our hearts still with him. Where we love most heartily, we will think most sweetly and most freely. Nothing will enliven our love for God more than our belief of his love to us. Therefore, get a truer understanding of the loving nature of God, store up all the experiences and discoveries of his love to you, and then see if it will not further your heavenly-mindedness.

9. Be a careful observer of the movements of the Spirit. Do not quench his motions or resist his workings. Heaven and your soul will be strangers to each other if the Spirit urges you to secret prayer and you refuse to obey, if he forbids your known transgressions and yet you continue in them, if he shows you which is the way and which not and you do not regard him. Do you not sometimes feel a strong impulse to retire from the world and draw near to God? Do not now disobey, but take up the offer and hoist your sail while you may have this blessed gale. When this wind blows strongest, you go fastest, either forward or backward. The more of this Spirit we resist, the deeper will it wound; the more we obey, the faster our pace.

10. Lastly, do not neglect the due care for the health of your body and for maintaining a vigorous cheerfulness in your spirits without pampering and indulging your flesh. Your body is a useful servant if you give it its due and only its due. It is a devouring tyrant if you allow it to have mastery or to have what it unreasonably desires. But do not deny what is necessary for its support, or it will be like a blunted knife or a horse that is lame. When we consider how frequently men offend on both extremes and how few use their bodies aright, we cannot be surprised if they are hindered in their heavenly conversing. You love

to have your knife sharp. How cheerfully you travel when your horse goes strongly. Thus your soul has need of a sound and cheerful body.

———

Questions for Reflection

1. Look back over the hindrances Baxter identifies. Which of them is a particular hindrance for you? How might you overcome it?

2. Which of Baxter's "positive helps" would provide you with the most encouragement? Are there any that you would not have thought of?

3. Baxter compares the heavenly life to climbing a mountain: we should not think we can "travel daily this steep ascent without a great deal of labor and resolution" (p. 111). Do you think he is right that practicing daily meditation on heaven will be hard work? Why or why not?

4. At this point in his book, how ready are you to pick up Baxter's challenge and resolve to develop a habit of heavenly-mindedness?

I Now Proceed to Direct
You in the Work

In the final third of the book, Baxter moves on from laying a long foundation to provide practical advice in the work of meditation. In this chapter he distinguishes the nature and focus of what he means by meditation; then he offers guidance on the fittest time and place for the work and how best to ready our hearts in preparation for it.

———

ALL I HAVE SAID so far is only the preparation for my principal end. Therefore, reader, if you neglect what now follows, you will frustrate the main end of my design. I entreat you to study the following directions and then speedily and faithfully put them into practice. Practice is the end of all sound doctrine, and all right faith ends in duty. Resolve before you read any further that no laziness of spirit will take you off or any lesser business interrupt your course but that you will prove yourself to be a doer of this word and not an idle hearer only (James 1:22).

Meditation is confessed to be a duty by all but denied by most in its constant neglect. Those who are very tender in their conscience toward most other duties too easily overlook this one as if they did not know it was a duty at all. They are troubled if they omit a sermon, a fast, or prayer, yet they are never troubled that they have omitted meditation perhaps all their lifetime to this very day. But this is the duty by which they will improve all those other duties. This is how the soul digests truths and draws forth their strength for its nourishment and refreshing. A man takes only half an hour in eating his food, but his body will take seven or eight hours at least to digest it. Just so, a man may take into his understanding and memory more truth in one hour than he is able to digest in many hours. A man may eat too much, but he cannot digest too well. Yet because "meditation" is a general word, and it is not all the meanings of the word that I here intend, I will now explain how the meditation I am urging is different from all other sorts of meditation.

The Definition of Meditation

Meditation entails *the set and solemn acting of all the powers of the soul*. I call it *set and solemn* to differentiate it from that which is only occasional and cursory. I charge you to make this meditation a constant, standing duty, just as you do in hearing, praying, and reading the Scripture. You should solemnly set yourselves to it—and while you do it, make it your whole work. Do not mix other matters in with it any more than you would do with prayer or other duties.

I call it the acting of *all* the powers of the soul to differentiate it from the common meditation of students, which usually involves only the mere employment of the brain. It is not a bare thinking that I intend by meditation but the business of a higher and more excellent nature. When truth is apprehended only as truth, this is but an unsavory and loose apprehension; when it is apprehended as good as well as true, this is a solid and delightful apprehending. As a man is not so prone to live according to the truth he knows unless it affects him deeply, so his soul does not enjoy its sweetness unless speculation passes to affection.

This has deceived too many Christians in this business. They have thought that meditation is nothing but the bare thinking on truths and the rolling of them in the understanding and memory. But any schoolboy can do this, even those who hate the subjects they think about. Therefore, this is the great task at hand, and this is the work that I would set you on: get these truths from your head to your heart. Take all the sermons that you have heard of heaven and all the notions that you have conceived of this rest, and turn them into the blood and spirits of affection so that you may feel them revive you and warm you at the heart. You will enjoy God only as much as you train your understanding and affections sincerely on him. That is the happy work of this meditation. So there is rather more to be done than merely remembering and thinking of heaven. Just as running and moving stir not only a hand or a foot but strain the whole body, so meditation exercises the whole soul.

Now you can see what this kind of meditation is: the set and solemn acting of all the powers of the soul. The object of this meditation is *rest*, or the most blessed condition of man in his everlasting enjoyment of God in heaven. Meditation in general has a large field to walk in. It has as many objects to work on as there are matters, lines, and words in the Scripture; as there are known creatures in the whole of creation; and as there are particular discernible workings of Providence throughout the world. But the meditation I now direct you in is only of the end of all these: our rest. It is not a walk from mountains to valleys, from sea to land, from kingdom to kingdom, from planet to planet. It is a walk from mountains and valleys to the holy Mount Zion, a walk from sea and land to the land of the living, a walk from the kingdoms of this world to the kingdom of saints, a walk from earth to heaven, a walk from time to eternity, a walk in the garden and paradise of God. That which will make us most happy when we possess it will make us most joyful when we meditate on it, especially when that meditation carries a degree of possession. That is exactly the meditation I here describe.

The Fittest Time and Place for Meditation

So far I have opened to you the nature of this duty of meditation, and by this point I suppose you partly apprehend what it is. I now proceed to direct you in the work. Begin by determining a set and constant time for meditation. As a craftsman in his shop will have a set place for every one of his tools and materials, so a Christian should have a set time for every ordinary duty. Otherwise, he is all too likely to neglect it. A stated time is a hedge to duty that defends against many temptations to omission.

Furthermore, make meditation a frequent duty. It is not for me to determine how often it should be, because men's conditions may vary. In general, it should be as frequent as the Scripture requires when it mentions meditating continually, day and night (Josh. 1:8; Ps. 1:2). Circumstances of our condition may vary the circumstances of our duties, but for those who can conveniently omit other business, I advise that it be once a day at least.

Three reasons especially should persuade you to frequency in this meditation on heaven. First, it will breed a strangeness between your soul and God if you converse with God only seldom. Frequent society breeds familiarity; familiarity increases love and delight and makes us bold and confident in our addresses. This is the main end of this duty, that you may have acquaintance and fellowship with God. Therefore, if you come to it only seldom, you will keep yourself a stranger and so miss out on the whole point of the work.

Second, meditating only occasionally will make you unskillful in the work. How clumsy men are when they set their hands to a work they are seldom employed in! But frequency will habituate your heart to the work, you will better know the way you walk every day, and it will be easier and more delightful to you. The hill that made you pant and blow when you first climbed up it, you may run up easily when you are once accustomed to it. The heart, which of itself is naturally backward, will contract a greater unwillingness through disuse.

Third, any heat and life you gain by this duty will be lost by long intermissions. If you eat only one or two meals in a few days, you will lose your strength as fast as you get it. In holy meditation you get near to Christ and warm your heart with the fire of love, but if you then turn away and come only on occasion, you will soon return to your former coldness.

I also advise you to choose the most seasonable time. I know that men's conditions of employment, freedom, and bodily temper are so varied that the same hour may be seasonable to one that is unseasonable to another. Every man is the fittest judge for himself. But let me offer the time I have always found fittest for myself, which is during the evening from sunset to the twilight, and sometimes in the night when it is warm and clear. I would not have mentioned my own experience except for the encouragement of finding that it matched the experience of a better and wiser man than myself. For it is said in Genesis 24:63 that Isaac went to meditate in the field during the evening, and his experience I more boldly recommend to you than my own. The Lord's Day is also a time that is exceedingly seasonable for this exercise. When could we more seasonably contemplate our rest than on that day of rest that pictures it for us?

These are the fittest seasons for the ordinary performance of this heavenly work, but there are special, particular times that are also seasonable. First, when God extraordinarily revives and enables your spirit, when he kindles your spirit with fire from above, it is then that your heart may mount aloft more freely. It is part of a Christian's skill to observe the gales of grace and how the Spirit of Christ moves upon his spirit. Without Christ we can do nothing (John 15:5). Therefore, let us be doing when he is doing and be sure not to be out of the way or asleep when he comes (Luke 12:37–38). The sails of the windmill do not stir without the wind; the workers must set them going when the wind blows. Be sure that you watch this wind and tide if you seek a speedy voyage to heaven.

Second, it is seasonable to address yourself to this duty when you are cast into perplexing troubles of mind through suffering, fear, care, or temptations. When is it more seasonable to walk to heaven than when we hardly know what corner on earth to live in with comfort? When should our thoughts converse above if not when they have nothing but grief to converse with below? Where should Noah's dove be if not in the ark when the waters cover all the earth and she cannot find rest for the sole of her foot (Gen. 8:9)? What should we think on if not our Father's house when we lack even the husks of the world to feed on (Luke 15:16–17)? God sends afflictions for this very purpose. Happy are you who are poor if you make this use of your poverty, and you who are sick if you so improve your sickness.

A third fit season for this heavenly duty is when the messengers of God summon us to die. When should we most frequently sweeten our souls with the believing thoughts of another life if not when we find that this life is almost at an end and when our flesh is raising fears and terrors? Surely no men have greater need of supporting joys than dying men, and those joys must be fetched from our eternal joy. As we say of the old and the weak, that they have one foot in the grave already, so may we say of the godly when they are near their rest: they have one foot, as it were, in heaven already. When should a traveler look homeward with joy if not when he comes within sight of his home? Oh, that we who are daily languishing could learn this daily, heavenly conversing (2 Cor. 4:16–18). Oh, that every gripe our bodies now feel might make us more sensible of our future ease, and that every weary day and hour might make us long for our eternal rest!

This much I thought necessary to advise you concerning the time of this duty, but let me now speak a little of the fittest place. As this is a private and spiritual duty, so it is most appropriate that you re-tire to some private place. Christ himself directed us in this private duty (Matt. 6:4, 6, 18). How often did he depart to some mountain, wilderness, or other solitary place (as in Mark 1:35)? I advise you to withdraw from all society, even the society of godly men, so that you may for a while enjoy the society of Christ.

Preparing Your Heart for Meditation

I will now give you some advice concerning the preparations of your heart. When you begin this duty, first get your heart as clear from the world as you can. Wholly set aside all thoughts of your business, your troubles, your enjoyments, and everything that might take up any room in your soul. Get your soul as empty as you possibly can so that it may be more capable of being filled with God. As I have said, it is a work that will require all the powers of your soul, even if they were a thousand times more capacious and active than they are.

Therefore, you will need to lay aside all other thoughts and affections while you are busy here.

Be sure you set upon this work with the greatest seriousness that you possibly can. Labor to have the deepest apprehensions of the presence of God and of the incomprehensible greatness of the majesty you approach. You are about to converse with him before whom the whole earth will quake and the devils tremble (James 2:19) and before whose bar of judgment you and all the world must shortly stand. Think to yourself, "I will then have lively apprehensions of his majesty. My drowsy spirits will then be awakened and my dull irreverence be laid aside. Why should I not now be roused with the sense of his greatness? Why should the dread of his name not possess my soul?"

Strive to apprehend the greatness of the work that you attempt and to be deeply sensible both of its weight and height. If the sun passes through an eclipse, how eagerly everyone runs out to see it. If an angel from heaven agreed to meet you at the same time and place of your contemplations, how dreadfully, how apprehensively would you go to meet him? Well then, consider with what a spirit you should meet the Lord and with what seriousness and dread you should daily converse with him.

Finally, consider the blessed fruit of the work if it succeeds. It will supply admission into the presence of God, a beginning of your eternal glory on earth, and a means to make you live above the rate of other men. It will admit you into the room next to the angels themselves. It will provide a means to make you live and die both joyfully and blessedly. Therefore, your preparations should be in proportion to the greatness of the prize.

———

Questions for Reflection

1. What do you make of Baxter's particular definition of meditation?

2. As Baxter says, most Christians accept that meditation is something God requires, yet most Christians do not practice it. Why is that? Are you one of those who do not make a habit of regular meditation?

3. "That which will make us most happy when we possess it will make us most joyful when we meditate on it" (p. 122). Can you see the advantages of this practice of meditating on our heavenly rest? How would your Christian experience be enhanced by it?

4. If you were to begin this practice, what would you choose as the time and place for doing it?

How to Fire Your Heart by the Help of Your Head

Baxter is nothing if not methodical. Here he lays out the main steps in his method of heavenly meditation. The key element is what he calls consideration: the art of reasoning with ourselves or persuading our hearts of the truth and joy of our everlasting rest. We employ our reason and our faith to lead our heart by the hand. In this way we stir up love, desire, hope, courage, and joy.

———

IT IS NOW TIME to direct you in the work of meditation and to show you the way to perform it. All that I have said so far has been merely to tune the instrument, your heart; now we come to the music itself. All this has been only to give you an appetite; now we come to the feast. Sit down, eat what is offered, and delight your soul. Whoever you are, if you are a child of the kingdom, I have this message to you from the Lord: Behold, the dinner is prepared, the oxen are killed, come, for all things are now ready (Matt. 22:4). Heaven is before you. Christ is before you. The eternal weight of glory is before you (2 Cor. 4:17). Come, therefore, and feed on it.

Employing Our Minds

In this chapter I will direct you how to use your understanding for the warming of your affections, how to fire your heart by the help of your head. The great instrument suited to this task is reasoning the case with yourselves. You might call this discourse of mind, cogitation, or thinking—or, if you will, call it *consideration*.

First, consideration opens the door between the head and the heart. The understanding stores truths in the memory; consideration conveys them to the affections. Man is a rational creature and apt to be moved in a reasoning way, especially when the reasons are evident and strong. Consideration is reasoning the case with one's own heart, and what a multitude of reasons both clear and weighty are always at hand to work on the heart! Matters of great weight that closely concern us work most effectually on the heart. Meditation brings out these working objects and presents them to the affections in their worth and weight.

When you are weighing something in the balance, you place a little more and then a little more until it weighs down. Likewise, if your affections hang in dull indifference, meditation will add reason after reason until the scales turn. Another man's reasons work powerfully with us even though we cannot be certain whether his heart agrees with his words or whether his intention is to inform us or deceive us. How much more should our own reasoning work with us when we are acquainted with the right intentions of our own hearts? How much more should God's reasons work with us when we can be certain they are false neither in his intent nor in themselves? Meditation is simply reading over and repeating God's reasons to our hearts and so disputing with ourselves in his arguments and terms. Observe how the prodigal son reasoned with himself why he should return to his father's house (Luke 15:17–19). We have just as many and just as strong reasons to urge on our affections to persuade them to seek our Father's everlasting habitations. It is by consideration that these reasons must all be set to work.

Meditation puts reason in its proper place of authority. It helps deliver reason from its captivity to the senses and sets it again on the throne of the soul. When reason is silent, it is usually subject, for when it is asleep, the senses dominate. Consideration awakens reason from its sleep until it rouses itself up like Samson and breaks the bonds of sensuality with which it is chained (Judg. 16:12). What strength can the lion put forth when he is asleep? What is a king more than any other man when he is deposed from his throne?

Thus you see what force meditation has to bring about this great elevation of the soul. Consideration must be the instrument.

Stirring Our Affections

To draw nearer the heart of the work, the next question is this: What sort of consideration is necessary to stir the affections?

1. You must go to your memory, the storehouse of the understanding, and fetch those heavenly doctrines you intend to make the subject of your meditation. For the present purpose you may choose any promise of eternal life or any description of the glory of the saints and the life everlasting. Even just one sentence concerning those eternal joys can provide you with subject matter for many years' meditation. We will be wise to always have a good stock of matter in our memory, so that when we use it, we can bring forth out of our treasury things new and old (Luke 6:45).

2. Your next task is to present to your judgment what you have retrieved from your memory. Open the case as fully as you can. Set forth the different ornaments of the crown and the many dignities of

the kingdom as they are partly laid open in the beginning of this book. Let your judgment deliberately and precisely survey them. Then put the question and require an answer: "Is there happiness in all this or not? Can he lack anything who fully possesses God? Is there anything higher for a creature to attain?" In this way, urge your judgment to pass a sentence, and compel it to subscribe to the perfection of your celestial happiness.

If your senses should here begin to mutter and to put in a word for fleshly pleasure or profits, let your judgment hear what each can say. Weigh the arguments of the world and flesh at one end and the arguments for the preeminence of glory at the other end, and judge impartially which should be preferred. Which is the more excellent? Which is the more satisfactory? Which is the more pure? Which brings the most freedom from misery? Which lasts longer? Let judgment decide, and when the sentence is passed and recorded in your heart, it will be ready to be produced on any future occasion to silence the flesh in its next attempt and to disgrace the world in its next competition.

3. The central work is to exercise your belief of the truth of your rest. This includes both the truth of the promise in itself and the truth of your own title to it. Oh, what passions it would raise within us if only we were thoroughly persuaded that every word in the Scripture concerning the inconceivable joys of the kingdom and the inexpressible blessedness of the life to come was the very word of the living God and will certainly be performed even to the smallest detail. If I were as truly persuaded that I will shortly see those great things of eternity promised in the word as I am that this is a chair I sit in or that this is paper I write on, would it not make me forget and despise the world? Therefore, let this be a chief part of your business in meditation.

Produce the strong arguments for the truth of Scripture; plead them against your unbelieving nature; answer and silence all the quibbling objections of infidelity.

Study also the gracious disposition of Christ and his readiness to entertain and welcome all who will come. Study all the evidences of his love that appeared in his sufferings, his preaching, his condescension to sinners, his easy conditions, his exceeding patience, and his urgent invitations. Do all these not demonstrate his readiness to save? Study also the evidence of his love in yourself. Look over the works of his grace in your soul. If you do not find the degree you would like, look for sincerity more than quantity.

Affections to Be Stirred

When your meditation has persuaded you of the truth of your happiness, the next task is to meditate on its goodness. When the judgment has determined and when faith has apprehended the truth of these things, you may then go on to raise the affections—in this order.

1. Love is the first affection to be stirred. The object of it, as I have told you, is goodness. Here then, Christian, is the soul-reviving part of your work. Bring forth the excellencies of everlasting rest from your memory, your judgment, and your faith, and present them to your affection of love. Let your faith, as it were, take your heart by the hand and show it the sumptuous buildings of your eternal habitation and the glorious ornaments of your Father's house. Let faith lead your heart into the presence of God, and say to it, "Behold, the ancient of days; the Lord Jehovah, whose name is 'I AM' (Ex. 3:14; Dan. 7:9). This is he who loved you from everlasting, who formed you in the womb and gave you this soul (Ps. 139:13–15). He maintains you with life, health, and comforts. Here, oh here, is an object worthy of your love. Here

you may be sure you cannot love too much. This is the Lord who has blessed you with his benefits, who has spread your table in the sight of your enemies and caused your cup to overflow (Ps. 23:5). This is he whom angels and saints praise and whom the host of heaven must magnify forever."

In this way you expound the praises of God to your own heart until you feel the life begin to stir and the fire in your breast begin to kindle. Just as gazing on the beauty of mere flesh kindles the fire of carnal love, so this gazing on the glory and goodness of the Lord will kindle this spiritual love in the soul.

Even though your heart is like rock and flint, striking often may bring forth the spark. So if you do not feel the stirrings of love, lead your heart further, and show it still more. Show it the Son of the living God, whose name is Wonderful Counselor, Mighty God, Everlasting Father, and Prince of Peace (Isa. 9:6). Show it the King of saints on the throne of his glory. He is the first and the last (Rev. 1:11), who is and was and is to come (Rev. 1:8). This is the one who was dead, and behold, he lives forevermore (Rev. 1:18). He has made your peace by the blood of his cross (Col. 1:20). Go on then, for the field of love is large. It will yield you fresh content forever and be your eternal work to behold and love. Thus I have shown you how to excite the affection of love.

2. Desire is the next affection to be excited, for if love is hot, desire will not be cold. So when you have viewed the goodness of the Lord, proceed with your meditation. Think with yourself, "Where have I been? What have I seen? Oh, the incomprehensible, astonishing glory! Oh, the rare, transcendent beauty! Oh, the blessed souls who now enjoy it, who see a thousand times more clearly what I have seen only darkly, at a distance, and hardly made out through the interposing

clouds (1 Cor. 13:12)! What a difference there is between my state and theirs. I am sighing, and they are singing. I am sinning, and they are pleasing God. I am here entangled in the love of the world, when they are taken up with the love of God. Oh, what a feast has my faith beheld, but oh, what a famine is still in my spirit! Why do I have to stay and groan and weep and wait? My Lord is gone. He has left this earth and entered into his glory. My friends are there; my house, my hope, my all is there; and must I stay behind to sojourn here?"

In this way, Christian reader, let your thoughts aspire. Whet the desires of your soul by these meditations until your soul longs to drink from the wells of salvation!

3. The next affection to be acted is hope, which is uniquely helpful to the soul. Hope helps support the soul in sufferings. Hope encourages the soul to venture on the greatest difficulties. Hope enlivens the soul in its duties. Hope is the spring that sets all the wheels in motion. Would the farmer plough and sow if he did not hope for the harvest? Would the soldier fight if he did not hope for victory? Therefore, Christian reader, when you are winding up your affections to heaven, remember to wind up your hope as well.

Reason with your own heart in this way: "Why should I not confidently and comfortably hope when my soul is in the hands of so compassionate a Savior? Did he ever show any reluctance to my good or demonstrate the least inclination to my ruin? How often has he drawn me to himself when I have drawn backward and would have broken from him? Look how he has pursued me from place to place. Would he have done all this if he had been willing that I should perish?" Thus you may stir up hope.

4. The next affection to be enlivened is courage. This boldness leads to resolution and concludes in action. So when you have stirred up

love, desire, and hope, go on and think further with yourselves: "Is there such a glory within the reach of hope? Oh, why do I not then lay hold of it? Where is the cheerful vigor of my spirit? Why do I not set upon my enemies on every side and valiantly break through all resistance? Why do I not take this kingdom by force (Matt. 11:12)? I have seen men daily in the wars venture upon armies, forts, and cannons, and cast themselves upon the instruments of death, and do I not have as fair a prize before me? Oh, blessed rest! Oh, most invaluable, glorious state! Who would sell you for dreams and shadows? Who would not strive, fight, watch, and run, even to the last breath, so that he might have this hope at the last to obtain you?" Thus you can see what kind of meditations may excite your courage and raise your resolutions.

5. The last affection to be acted is joy. This is the end of all those who came before. Love, desire, hope, and courage all tend to the raising of our joy. By this point, if you have managed well the former work, you have come within sight of your rest. You believe the truth of it, you are convinced of the excellency of it, you have fallen in love with it, you long after it, you hope for it, and you are resolved courageously to venture forth to obtain your rest. But is there any work for joy in this? You might say, "Alas, I am yet without my rest." Well, think a little further with yourself: "Though the actual possession will afford the highest joy, the imperfect idea or image in my understanding can still afford me a great deal of true delight. Is it nothing to have a deed of gift from God? Are his infallible promises no ground of joy? Is it nothing to live in daily expectation of entering into the kingdom? Is my assurance of being glorified one of these days not a sufficient ground for inexpressible joy? Am I not commanded to 'rejoice in hope of the glory of God' (Rom. 5:2)?"

Reader, take your heart once again and lead it by the hand. Bring it to the top of the highest mountain. Show it the kingdom of Christ and the glory of it. Say to your heart, "All this will your Lord bestow on you. It is the Father's good pleasure to give you this kingdom (Luke 12:32). Do you see the astonishing glory above you? This is your own inheritance! This crown is yours. These pleasures are yours. This company is yours. This beauteous place is yours. All things are yours, because you are Christ's and Christ is yours."

Proceed still further on. The soul who loves will ascend frequently to run through the streets of the heavenly Jerusalem, visiting the patriarchs and prophets, saluting the apostles, and admiring the armies of martyrs and confessors. Lead on your heart from street to street. Bring it into the palace of the great King. Lead it from chamber to chamber and say to it, "Here I will live, here I will praise, here I will love and be loved. Among this blessed company I will take my place. My tears will then be wiped away (Rev. 21:4), and my groans will be turned to another tune. My cottage of clay will be changed to this palace, and my prison rags to these splendid robes. Oh, when I look on this glorious place, what a dunghill and dungeon the earth starts to seem. Oh, what a difference there is between a man who is feeble, pained, groaning, dying, rotting in the grave and one of these triumphant, blessed, shining saints. Here I will drink of the streams that make glad the city of our God, and the Lord will rejoice in his people (Ps. 46:4; Isa. 65:19)." And thus, reader, I have directed you how to awaken your joy.

You do not have to stir these affections in exactly this order or all on the one occasion. Sometimes you may feel that one of your affections is flatter than the others, and so you might think it more seasonable to help that one forward alone. Or if your time is short, you might work on one affection one day and another the next as you find cause. All this I leave to your own prudence.

———

Questions for Reflection

1. Baxter demonstrates an orderly way of working that employs our minds to stir up our hearts in each of those five affections. What do you think of his framework?

2. Do you agree that how we talk to ourselves has a powerful effect on our spiritual and emotional state? How do you talk to yourself? Is heaven a regular part of that conversation?

3. "Even though your heart is like rock and flint, striking often may bring forth the spark" (p. 134). Do you have a rocky heart? How might you use Baxter's method to coax it into flame?

4. In this chapter you have overheard Baxter talking to himself. What do you notice about his conversation? Is there anything for you to emulate?

The Most Difficult Part of the Work

The work of heavenly meditation that Baxter describes has, as we have seen, many obstacles and hindrances. Not the least of these is our own heart. It is far more easily taken in with the desires of our natural senses than it is by the more remote but far more compelling vision of heavenly delight and joy. Baxter's solution is to employ our senses in the work of firing our hearts toward heaven and to bring our hearts under a firm hand.

———

CHRISTIAN READER, I will now show you what advantages and helps you should use to make your meditation on heaven more sweet and lively. This is the whole point: that you do not stop at bare thinking or consideration but have the lively sense of all on your hearts. You will find this to be the most difficult part of the work. It is easier to think about heaven for a whole day than to be lively and affectionate in those thoughts for a quarter of an hour. Therefore, consider a little further what may be done to make your thoughts of heaven to be piercing, affecting, and raising thoughts.

Using Our Senses to Aid Our Faith

Here you must understand that the work of faith has many disadvantages in comparison with the work of sense. Faith is imperfect, for we are renewed only in part, but sense has its strength according to the strength of the flesh. Faith goes against a world of resistance, but sense does not. Faith is supernatural and therefore prone to declining. It tends to languish even when it is being renewed and revived. But sense is natural and therefore continues as long as nature continues. The object of faith is far off: we must go as far as heaven for our joys. But the object of sense is close at hand. It is no easy matter to rejoice at what we have not seen, upon a mere promise written in the Bible, but it is very easy to rejoice in what we already see, feel, and possess.

Well then, what should be done in this case? We should call on the assistance of our sense. If we can make friends of what is usually our enemy and make it the instrument of raising us to God, I think we will perform a very excellent work. Surely it is possible, lawful, and, yes, even necessary to do this. God would not have given us our different senses if they could not be put in service to raise us up to the apprehension of higher things. Consider how the Holy Spirit condescends in the phrasing of Scripture to bring things down to the reach of our sense. He sets forth the excellence of spiritual things in words that are borrowed from the objects of sense. In particular, he describes the glory of the New Jerusalem in expressions that might appeal even to flesh itself: the streets and buildings are pure gold, the gates are pearl, and a throne stands in the midst of the city (Rev. 21–22). We will eat and drink with Christ at his table in his kingdom (Luke 22:30). He will drink with us the fruit of the vine anew (Matt. 26:29). These, with most other descriptions of our glory, even though only figurative, are expressed as if they were to our flesh and sense.

Imagine that you are even now beholding this city of God. You stand with John to survey the thrones, the majesty, the heavenly hosts, the shining splendor that he saw (Rev. 4:1–2). Now draw the strongest impressions from your sense that you can for the stirring of your affections. Imagine that you hear all creatures praising and glorifying the living God (Rev. 5:13). Even now, you see all the saints in their white robes with palms in their hands (Rev. 7:9). You can hear those songs of Moses and of the Lamb (Rev. 15:3). Get the liveliest picture of them in your mind that you possibly can. Meditate on them as if you were actually beholding them, as if you were hearing the hallelujahs while you think of them. Go on until you can say, "I see a glimpse of the glory! I hear the shouts of joy and praise! I stand beside Abraham, David, Peter, Paul, and many more of these triumphing souls! I even see the Son of God appearing in the clouds (Matt. 24:30) and the world standing before him to receive their doom. I hear him say, 'Come, you blessed of my Father!' (Matt. 25:34), and I see them go rejoicing into the joy of their Lord!"

Comparing Objects of Sense with Objects of Faith

We can make our senses serviceable to us by comparing the objects of our senses with the objects of faith. I will now set forth the various ways in which you might do this.

1. Compare the delights of the saints in heaven with the corrupt delights of sensual men. Think with yourself, "If it is such a delight to a sinner when he does sinful things, will it not be delightful indeed to live with God? The drunkard has so much delight in his drink and companions that even the fear of damnation will not make him forsake them. Surely, then, there are higher delights with God. If the way to hell can afford such pleasure, what are the pleasures of the saints in

heaven? If the covetous man has so much pleasure in his wealth, and the ambitious man has such pleasure in his power and titles of honor, what pleasure, then, will the saints have in the everlasting treasures? What pleasure will we receive when we will be set above principalities and powers and made the glorious spouse of Christ?"

2. Compare the delights above with the lawful delights of our senses in their moderation. Think with yourself, "How sweet is food to my taste when I am hungry? Oh, what delight, then, will my soul have in feeding on Christ, the living bread, and in eating with him at his table in his kingdom (Luke 22:30)? How pleasant is drink in the extremity of thirst? Think, then, how delightful it will be to my soul to drink of that fountain of living water. Wine is so pleasant and refreshing that it is said to make glad the heart of man (Ps. 104:15). How pleasant, then, will that wine of the great marriage be?" Consider how delightful each pleasant fragrance is to our sense of smell, how delightful perfect music is to our ear, how delightful beautiful sights are to our eye. Every time you see or remember these delights, think of the fragrant smell of the precious ointment poured on the head of our glorified Savior, which will also be poured on the heads of all his saints. Think how delightful the music of the heavenly host will be and how pleasing true beauty will be.

3. Compare also the excellence of heaven with the glorious works of the creation that our eyes now behold. A great deal of wisdom, power, majesty, and goodness appears in them to a wise observer. This makes the study of the natural world so pleasant, because the works of God are so excellent. What rare workmanship is in the body of a man and even in the body of every beast? What excellence lies in every plant we see, in the beauty of flowers, and in the nature, diversity, and use of herbs, fruit, or roots? If we consider the whole body of this earth and

its inhabitants, the ocean of waters with its motions and dimensions, the variation of the seasons and of the face of the earth, what wonderful excellence do they all contain? Think, therefore, in your meditations, that if these things that are only servants to sinful men are so full of mysterious worth, then what is that place where God himself dwells that is prepared for the just, who are perfected with Christ?

4. Compare the things that you will enjoy above with the excellence of those admirable works of providence that God brings about in the church and in the world. What glorious things the Lord has wrought, and yet we will see more glorious than these. If we observe everyday providences, they are all very admirable: the movement of the sun, the tides of the sea, the warming of the earth, the watering of it with rain as if it were a garden, the keeping of a wicked and confused world in order, with multitudes of other instances like these. Now think of the Zion of God, of the vision of the divine majesty, of the pleasing order of the heavenly host. What an admirable sight that must be! Oh, what rare and mighty works have we seen in these last four or five years of civil war. What changes, what subduing of enemies, what clear discoveries of an almighty arm, what turning of tears and fears into safety and joy, what hearing of earnest prayers, as if God could have denied us nothing that we asked! All these were wonderful heart-raising works. But what are they compared to our full deliverance, our final conquest, our eternal triumph?

5. Compare the mercies you will have above with the works of providence that you have enjoyed yourself and recorded through your life. Look over the excellent mercies of your youth and education, the mercies of your more mature years, and the mercies of your prosperity and of your adversity. Are they not excellent and innumerable? How sweet was it to you when God resolved your doubts, when he silenced

your fears and unbelief, when he prevented the inconveniences of your life that your own wisdom would have cast you into, when he eased your pains and healed your sickness. All these were precious mercies, yet they are as nothing compared to the mercies above. If my pilgrimage and warfare have such mercies, what will I find in my home and in my triumph? If God communicates so much to me while I remain a sinner, what will he bestow when I am a perfect saint? If I have had so much in this strange, distant country, what will I have in his immediate presence, where I will forever stand about his throne?

6. Compare the comforts you will have above with the supports of faith you receive here. Has the word been to you as an open fountain, flowing with comforts day and night? Think, then, that if the word is so full of consolations, what overflowing springs will we find in God? If his letters are so comfortable, how much more the words that flow from his blessed lips? How often have you joined with your congregation troubled in spirit but returned home in quietness and delight? Well then, if the very feet of the messengers of these tidings of peace are beautiful (Isa. 52:7), how beautiful is the face of the Prince of Peace (Isa. 9:6)? If the word in the mouth of a fellow servant is so pleasant, how much more the living Word himself? If this treasure is so precious in earthen vessels (2 Cor. 4:7), how much more the treasure laid up in heaven? Consider the consolation you have received in the Lord's Supper and what a privilege it is to be admitted to sit at his table. Oh, the difference between the Last Supper of Christ on earth and the Marriage Supper of the Lamb at the great day (Rev. 19:6–9)! Think what a joy it is here, when anything ails you, to go to God and open your soul to him as if to your most faithful friend, especially when you know his ability and willingness to relieve you. It will be a more unspeakable joy when you will receive all blessings without asking

for them, when all your necessities and miseries are removed, and when God himself will be the portion and inheritance of your soul.

7. Compare the glory of the heavenly kingdom with the glory of the imperfect church on earth and with the glory of Christ in his state of humiliation. If, when he rises again, the grave and death have lost their power, if the bolted doors cannot keep him out (John 20:19), if he can ascend to heaven in the sight of his disciples (Acts 1:9), what power, dominion, and glory does he now possess? We will forever possess that glory with him! If the very preaching of the gospel be accompanied with such power that it will pierce the heart, bring down the proud, and make the stony sinner tremble, what then will be the glory of the kingdom itself? If the saints have this power and honor in the time appointed for their suffering and disgrace, what power and honor will they have in their full advancement?

8. Compare the glorious change that you will have at last with the gracious change that the Spirit has already wrought on your heart. If we are said to be like God and to bear his image while we are still pressed down with a body of sin, surely we will then be much more like God when we are perfectly holy and without blemish (Eph. 5:27; Jude 1:24) and have no such thing as sin within us. If our joy in foreseeing and believing is so sweet, how much more will we enjoy our full possession?

And thus I have shown you how to get your meditations to enliven your affections by comparing the unseen delights of heaven with those smaller pleasures you have seen and felt in the flesh.

Managing Our Hearts

Finally, I will guide you how to manage your heart through this work and show you how you need to be exceedingly watchful. For you will find that your own heart will be your greatest hinderer. It will prove false to you in one or all of these four ways.

1. You will find your heart as backward to this as to any work in the world. Oh, what excuses and evasions it will offer! What is to be done? Well, what would you do to a servant or a horse that draws back when you require him to go forward? You would first persuade, then chide, then spur him, and then force him on. You would take no denial. You would not leave him alone until he had completed his work. In the same way, set upon your heart and persuade it to the work. Take no denial. Chide it for its backwardness. Use violence with it. Bring it into service, willing or not. Are you master of your flesh, or are you a servant to your flesh? Have you no command of your own thoughts? Can your will not choose the subject of your meditations? If you are too weak for the task, call the Spirit of Christ to your assistance. He is never backward to so good a work, nor will he deny his help in so just a cause. By doing this, you will see your heart submit. Its resistance and backwardness will be turned to a yielding compliance.

2. When you have gotten your heart to do the work, beware lest it deceive you with a loitering formality. Do not let it trifle out the time while it should be effectually meditating. When you have only an hour for your meditation, the time will be spent before your heart has even begun to be serious. To run out the hour in a bare, lazy thinking of heaven is only to lose that hour and delude yourself. What is to be done? Exactly what you would do with a loitering servant: keep your eye always on your heart. Do not look so much to the time it spends in the duty as to the quantity and quality of the work that it does. You can tell by his work whether your servant has been careful. Ask yourself, "What affections have yet to be stirred? How much am I yet to get nearer to heaven?" Truly, many a man's heart must be followed

as closely in this duty of meditation as an ox at the plough that will go on no longer than you are calling or scourging. If you cease driving even for a moment, your heart will stand still. Even the best hearts have much of this temper.

3. As your heart will too quickly loiter, so it will too easily be distracted. It will turn aside like a careless servant to talk with everyone who passes by. When there should be nothing in your mind but the work at hand, your heart will be thinking of your calling; of your afflictions; of every bird, tree, or place that you see; or of any other subject at all rather than that of heaven. Experience shows that you will have great difficulty keeping your heart to the work without many idle thoughts distracting it. The cure here is the same: to use watchfulness and violence with your own imaginations, and as soon as they step outside, to chide them back in. Say to your heart, "Did I come here to think of my business in the world, to think of places, persons, news, or vanity, or of anything else but heaven, be it never so good? Can you not watch even for one hour (Matt. 26:40)? Do you hope to leave this world and dwell with Christ forever, and yet you cannot leave it for one hour out of your thoughts, nor dwell with Christ in one hour's close meditation?"

4. Be sure to look to your heart that it does not end the work before the time and does not run away through weariness before you have given it leave. You will find it will be exceedingly prone to this. As fast as you get up your heart, it will be down again. It will weary of the work. It will remind you of other business to be done. It will stop your heavenly walk before you are fully warm. What is to be done in this case? The same authority and resolution that brought your heart to the work and observed it in the work must also hold your heart until the work is done. Charge it in the name of God to stay. Say to it, "Foolish heart! If you

stop before you are at the end of your journey, is not every step of your travel lost? You came here hoping to catch a sight of the glory you will inherit, and will you stop when you are almost at the top of the hill and turn back down before you have taken in the view? You came here in the hope of speaking with God, and will you leave before you have heard his voice? You came to bathe yourself in the streams of consolation, and to that end you took off the clothes of your earthly thoughts, and will you only dip in a toe and be gone so soon?" Stick, therefore, to the work until your affections are raised and your soul refreshed with the delights above. "Blessed is that servant whom his Lord, when he comes, will find so doing" (Matt. 24:46).

Questions for Reflection

1. It is surely true that our senses drive us more easily than our faith does. What do you make of Baxter's advice to employ our senses to aid our faith?

2. What comparison do you draw between the pleasures and provision you experience here and the joy and plenty of heaven? Is that sufficient motivation for you to contemplate heaven in a more intentional way? Why or why not?

3. "Experience shows that you will have great difficulty keeping your heart to the work without many idle thoughts distracting it" (p. 147). Is that your experience? What will you do to manage your heart?

4. Baxter has provided help and advice in the work of heavenly meditation. Which pieces of advice do you find most beneficial?

Preaching to Oneself

In this final chapter, Baxter allows us to listen in on how he speaks to himself in heavenly meditation. He calls this practice soliloquy, which means speaking to oneself. Soliloquy is the conversation that goes on in our own head. Baxter's method brings discipline, shape, and focus to that conversation—in this case, a focus on rest—in a way that stirs up the affections of love, joy, desire, and hope. We now get to hear how he put his method into practice.

———

WE HAVE SEEN that the first and main instrument of this work of meditation is consideration and that consideration by itself will not pierce and affect the heart. We must go further to stir up each of our affections. The way we do that is through soliloquy. This is where we plead the case with our own souls.

The Place of Soliloquy

Soliloquy has been the practice of God's people in all times. Observe, for example, how David pleaded with his soul and argued it into a holy confidence and comfort in Psalms 42 and 43: "Why are you cast down, oh my soul, and why are you in turmoil within me? Hope in God, for I will yet praise him, who is the health of my countenance and my God" (Ps. 43:5). We see soliloquy also in Psalm 103:1–2, "Bless the Lord, oh my soul, and all that is within me, . . . and forget not all his benefits." So this is no new path I persuade you to tread but one that the saints have always used in their meditation.

Soliloquy has its component parts and its due method in which we stir up our affections one by one. I cannot attempt to explain either parts or method fully because it would take up more time and room than I intend or can allow it. But I will say this much in brief: just as every good master and father of a family is a good preacher to his own family, so every good Christian is a good preacher to his own soul. Soliloquy is preaching to oneself. Therefore, the very same method a minister uses when he preaches to others is what a Christian should use when speaking to himself. Do you understand the best method for a preacher? Observe the most affecting, heart-melting minister, and set him before you as a pattern to follow. Consider how he moves the hearts of his people, and take the same way with your own heart.

I will now give you an example of how you might preach to yourself from the verse before us: "There remains therefore a rest for the people of God" (Heb. 4:9).

Speaking to One's Own Heart

Rest! How sweet a word is this to my ears? Rest! Not as the stone rests on the earth or as these clods of flesh will rest in their grave. Nor is this such a rest as the carnal world desires. No, no, we have a different kind of rest from these. We will rest from all our labors, which were only ever the way and the means to rest. Yet even that is only the smallest part. Oh, blessed rest, where we will never rest day or night, crying, "Holy, holy, holy, Lord God of Sabbaths!" We will rest from sin but not from worship, from suffering and sorrow but not from solace! Oh, blessed day, when I will rest with God, when I will rest in knowing, loving, rejoicing, and praising, when my perfect soul and body together will perfectly enjoy the most perfect God! This God, who is love itself, will perfectly love me! He will rest in his love for me just as I will rest in my love for him. He will rejoice over me with singing (Zeph. 3:17), as I will rejoice in him. How near is that most blessed, joyful day? Though my Lord seems to delay his coming, yet a little while, and he will be here (Heb. 10:37).

Oh my soul, look ahead to that day. Do you regret your sufferings and sorrows now, your self-denying and holy walking? See how the judge smiles on you! There is love in his eyes. Listen, does he not call you? He bids you stand here at his right hand. Do not fear, for that is where he sets his sheep. Oh, joyful sentence pronounced by that blessed mouth: "Come, you who are blessed by my Father, inherit the kingdom prepared for you from the foundation of the world" (Matt. 25:34). See how your Savior takes you by the hand. The door is open, the kingdom is his—and therefore yours. There is your place before his throne. The Father receives you as the spouse of his Son. He welcomes you with the crown of glory (1 Pet. 5:4).

This was the aim of free, redeeming grace, this the purpose of eternal love. This joy was purchased by sorrow; this crown was obtained by the cross. My Lord wept so that now my tears might be wiped away. He was forsaken so that I might not now be forsaken. He died so that I might now live. This weeping, wounded Lord will I behold. This bleeding Savior will I see. I will live in him who died for me. Oh, free mercy that can exalt so vile a wretch—free to me but dear to Christ.

Oh, blessed grace! Oh, blessed love! Oh, the frame that my soul will then be in! Oh, how love and joy will stir! But I cannot express it. I cannot conceive it.

See the happy reunion with my old friends with whom I prayed, wept, and suffered. We spoke together of this day and place! The grave could not contain you. The same love has redeemed and saved you as well. This is not like our cottages of clay, our prisons, our earthly dwellings. This voice of joy is not like our old complaints, our groans, our sighs, our impatient moans. This body is not like the body we had, nor this soul like the soul we had, nor this life like the life we then lived. We have changed our place, our state, our clothes, our thoughts, our looks, our language.

Oh, what a blessed change this is! Farewell, sin and suffering forever. Farewell, my hard and rocky heart. Farewell, my proud and unbelieving heart. Farewell, my idolatrous and worldly heart. Farewell, my sensual and carnal heart. And now welcome, most holy and heavenly nature. As it must be employed in beholding the face of God, so is it full of God alone and delighted in nothing else but him.

Ah, my drowsy, earthy, blockish heart! How coldly you think of this reviving day! Do you sleep when you think of eternal rest? Are you leaning earthward when heaven is before you? Would you rather sit down in the dirt and dung than walk in the court of the palace of God? Come away! Make no excuse, make no delay. God commands you, and I command you: Come away! Gird up your loins, ascend the mountain, and look about you with seriousness and with faith. Do not look back toward the way of the wilderness, unless your eyes are so dazzled with glory that you desire to compare this kingdom with that howling desert and more sensibly perceive the mighty difference between them.

Stirring Love

Draw nearer yet, then, oh my soul. Here's something truly worth your loving. If love deserves love, what incomprehensible love is here before you? Even if you were to pour out the full store of your affections, it would be too little. Oh, that it were more. Oh, that it were many thousand times more! What a sea of love lies before you. Throw yourself in. Swim with the arms of your love in this ocean of his love.

Lord, how should I return love for so much love? Can I love as high, as deep, as broad, or as long as love itself? Can I love as much as he who made me—and who made me love? As I cannot match you in the works of your power, nor make, nor preserve, nor guide the worlds, why should I think of matching you in love? No, Lord, I yield. I am unable. I am overcome. Oh, blessed conquest! Go on victoriously, and still prevail and triumph in your love. This captive of love will proclaim your victory. When you lead me in triumph from earth to heaven, from death to life, from the bar of judgment to the throne, I and all who see it will acknowledge that you have prevailed. All will say, "Behold how he loved him" (John 11:36).

Stirring Joy

Awake then, oh my drowsy soul! Sit no longer by the fire of earthly comforts, driven by the cold of carnal fears and sorrows. Your winter is past. Will you still house yourself in earthly thoughts and confine yourself to drooping and dullness? Even the silly flies will leave their holes when the winter is over and the sun draws near. The ants will stir, the fish will rise, the birds will sing, the earth will look green, and all these with joyful note will tell you that spring has arrived. Come forth then, oh my drooping soul, and lay aside your mourning robes of winter. Let it be seen in your believing joys and praise that the day is appearing and spring has come. Now you see the green shoots of your comforts, but you will shortly see them white and ripe for harvest. You who are now called forth to see and taste will then be called forth to reap and gather. Will I delay my joys until then? Should the joys of the spring not go before the joys of harvest? Away then, you soul-tormenting cares and fears! Away, you complaining, heart-vexing sorrows! At least spare me a little while. Stay here below while I go up to see my rest.

Oh, what a blessed day that will be when I will have all mercy, the perfection of mercy, nothing but mercy, and fully enjoy the Lord of mercy himself! When I will stand on the shore and look back on the raging seas that I have safely passed through. When I will in full possession of glory look back on all my pains and troubles, all my fears and tears, and all the mercies that I received during my pilgrimage, and will then behold the glory that is the end of all this. Oh, what a blessed view will that be! Oh, the glorious prospect that I will have on the celestial Mount Zion! How could my heart not be raised in perfect joy when I am so raised? If one drop of lively faith were mixed with these considerations, oh, what a heaven-ravished heart I would carry within me! I dearly would believe; Lord, help my unbelief (Mark 9:24).

But alas, I am at a loss in the midst of my contemplations. I thought my heart all this while had followed after me, but I see it did not. Will I let my understanding go on alone or my tongue run on without affections? What life lies in empty thoughts and words? Neither God nor I find pleasure in them. Instead, let me turn back again to seek, find, and chide this lazy, loitering heart that turns away from such a pleasant work as this. Where have you been, unworthy heart, while I was opening to you the everlasting treasures? Did you sleep? Were you minding something else? Do you think that all this is but a dream or a fable? Or have you lost your life and rejoicing power? Oh Lord, what is the matter that this work goes on so heavily? Is my heart really so reluctant to rejoice? I have been lifting this stone, and it will not stir. I hope, Lord, by the time it comes to heaven, that this heart will be enlivened and mended by your Spirit.

Stirring Desire

Besides my darkness, deadness, and unbelief, I perceive there is something else that prevents my full joy: this is not the time or the place for perfect joy. This is our wintertime, not our harvest. This is the valley of tears. There must necessarily be a great difference between the way and the end, the work and wages, the small foretastes and the final, full fruition. Even so, Lord, though you have reserved our joys for heaven, you have not suspended our desires. They are most suitable and seasonable in this present life. Therefore, help me desire until I may possess. There is love in desire as well as in delight, and if I am not empty of love, I know I will not long be empty of delight. Rouse yourself up once more then, oh my soul, and exercise your spiritual appetite.

Stirring Hope

How then should I long for my full recovery when there is no sickness, pain, weeping, or complaints? When will I arrive at that safe and quiet harbor where there are none of these storms and dangers? When will I never again face a weary, restless night or day? Then my life will not be such a mixture of hope and fear, of joy and sorrow, as it is now. Flesh and spirit will no longer be fighting within me, nor my soul be the site of a pitched battle where faith and unbelief, engagement and distrust, humility and pride, maintain a continual, distracting conflict. I will then no longer live a dying life for fear of dying, nor will my life be made uncomfortable with the fear of losing it. Oh, when will I be past these soul-tormenting fears and cares, these griefs and passions! When will I be out of this frail, corruptible, ruinous body; this soul-contradicting, ensnaring, deceiving flesh; and this vain, vexatious world!

In our current misery we long for peace. Why then am I not more weary of this weariness? Why do I so easily forget my resting place? Awake then, oh my drowsy soul, and look above this world of sorrows! Why do you linger here? Up and away! Have you forgotten that certain prediction of your Lord, "In the world you will have trouble, but in me you will have peace" (John 16:33)? The first you have found to be true by long experience, and of the latter you have had a small foretaste, but the perfect peace is still ahead of you.

A Concluding Prayer

What interest has this empty world for me? What is there that seems so lovely as to entice my desires and delight from you, oh God, or make me reluctant to come away with you? When I look around with a deliberate, undeceived eye, I perceive that this world is a howling wilderness and that most of the inhabitants are untamed, hideous monsters. All its beauty I can wink into blackness, and all its mirth I can think into sadness. I can drown all its pleasures in a few penitent tears, and the wind of a sigh will scatter them away. When I look on them without the spectacles of flesh, I call them nothing. They are mere vanity—or worse than nothing, a vexation. Oh, do not let this flesh so seduce my soul as to make it prefer this weary life before the joys that are about your throne!

Though death in itself is unwelcome to nature, may your grace make your glory appear so desirable that death may seem the messenger of my joy. Do not allow my soul to be ejected by violence and dispossessed of its habitation against its will, but draw it forth to yourself by the secret power of your love, as the sunshine in the spring draws forth the creatures from their winter holes. Meet it halfway, and entice it to you as the magnet draws the iron and as the greater flame attracts the lesser. Dispel, therefore, the clouds that hide your love from me. Remove the scales that hinder my eyes from beholding you. For only the beams of light that stream from your face and the foretaste of your great salvation can make a soul honestly say, "Now let your servant depart in peace" (Luke 2:29).

Oh, do not allow me to spend another day in strangeness and averseness to you while I endure my pilgrimage. While I have a thought to think, do not let me forget you. While I have a tongue to move, let me speak of you with delight. While I have a breath to breathe, let it be after you and for you. While I have a knee to bend, let it bow daily at your feet.

Let me die the death of the righteous (Num. 23:10). Let my last end be like his, even a removal to that glory that will never end. Send forth your convoy of angels for my departing soul, and let them bring me among the perfected spirits of the just (Heb. 12:23). Let me follow my dear friends who have died in Christ before me. When my friends are weeping over my grave, let my spirit repose with you in rest. And when my corpse lies rotting in the dark, let my soul be in the inheritance of the saints in light.

Oh, hasten that great resurrection day, when your command will go forth and none will disobey, when the sea and earth will yield up their hostages and all who sleep in their graves will awake and the dead in Christ will rise first, when the seed that you sowed corruptible will come forth incorruptible and the graves that received nothing but rottenness and retained nothing but dust will return to you glorious stars and suns. Therefore, I dare to lay down my carcass in the dust, entrusting it not to a grave but to you. My flesh will rest in hope until you raise it up to the full possession of the saints' everlasting rest.

———

Questions for Reflection

1. Do you agree with Baxter that "soliloquy has been the practice of God's people in all times" (p. 149)? Why or why not?

2. We are constantly talking to ourselves whether we recognize it or not, and Baxter encourages us to methodically and intentionally change the conversation. What impact do you think it would have on your own internal conversation if you followed his advice?

3. What do you notice about the way Baxter talks to himself? Is there anything in here for you to emulate? Could you talk to yourself in a similar way?

4. As the chapter goes on, Baxter turns increasingly from addressing his own soul to addressing God. What is the relationship between the method of meditation he is urging and the practice of prayer?

Conclusion

Baxter brings his book to a close with a few brief thoughts and a final challenge. As someone who has practiced daily heavenly meditation for years, he advertises the benefits from personal experience and laments how few Christians commit to the practice. He now challenges us to believe him on the benefits of meditation and to resolve to put his method into practice.

———

THUS, DEAR READER, I have given you my best advice for attaining and maintaining a heavenly life. The manner is imperfect and too much my own, but for the substance of the matter, I daresay that I received it from God. From him I deliver it to you, and his charge I lay on you, that you entertain and practice it. If you cannot do it methodically and fully, do it as best you can—only be sure you do it seriously and frequently. You will find that it will change you completely. It will elevate your soul, clear your understanding, and leave a pleasant savor in your heart. Your own experience will make you confess that one hour spent in heavenly meditation will more effectually revive you than many hours in bare, external duties. A day in these contemplations will bring you more contentment than all the glory and riches of the earth.

Be acquainted with this work, and you will, in some small, remote way, be acquainted with God. Your joys will be spiritual, prevalent, and lasting, according to the nature of their blessed object. You will have comfort in life and comfort in death. When you have neither wealth, nor health, nor the pleasure of this world, yet you will have comfort: a comfort without the presence or help of any friend, without a minister, without a book; when all means are denied you or taken from you, even then you may have vigorous, real comfort. You will be like one who stands at the top of an exceedingly high mountain. He looks down on the world as if it were quite below him. How small do the fields and woods seem to him? Cities and towns seem like only tiny spots. That is how you will look on all things here below. The greatest princes will seem merely as grasshoppers, and the busy, contentious, covetous world only as a heap of ants. Men's threats will hold no terror for you, nor the honors of this world any strong appeal. Temptations will be more harmless, having lost their strength; afflictions will be less grievous, having lost their sting; and every mercy will be better known and relished.

Alas, how little do many godly Christians differ from the world, either in where they seek their comforts or in their willingness to die, and all because they live as strangers to the true place and fountain of their comforts. Besides fulfilling a few duties, debating the doctrines of religion, or forbearing the practice of many sins, how little do most Christians differ from other men when God has prepared so vast a difference hereafter. If a word of heaven falls into their conversation now and then, how slight, customary, and heartless it is. If their prayers or preaching carry heavenly expressions, they are usually fetched from their mere invention, memory, or books, and not from the experience or feeling of their hearts. Oh, what a life might men live if only they were willing and diligent in this heavenly life! How much do those

Christians wrong God and themselves who let these offered joys lie neglected or forgotten?

What do you say? Do you resolve on this heavenly course or not? Will you let go of all your sinful, fleshly pleasures and daily seek after these higher delights? Shut the book now. Consider the matter, and resolve on the duty before you go any further. Let your family perceive, let your neighbors perceive, let your conscience perceive—yes, let God perceive—that you are one who will have your daily conversation in heaven.

But for you, sincere believers, whose hearts God has weaned from all things here below, I hope you will value this heavenly life and fetch one walk every day in the new Jerusalem. I know God is your love and your desire. I know you yearn to be more acquainted with your Savior. I know it is your grief that your hearts are not nearer to him and that they do not love him with more feeling, passion, and delight. If ever you would have all this mended and enjoy your desires, try this life of meditation on your everlasting rest!

Questions for Reflection

1. Baxter claims that the daily practice of meditation on heaven will change one's life completely. Do you think that is possible? Is it worth finding out? Why or why not?

2. Baxter observes that Christians do not differ all that much from their neighbors. Most Christians are content to focus their energies and attention on the things of earth, with little thought of heaven. How important is it to you that the same thing will not be said of you?

3. Having read the whole book, how would you summarize Baxter's message in a few sentences?

4. How do you respond to his final challenge: "What do you say? Do you resolve on this heavenly course or not?" (p. 161)? What will be your "heavenly course"?

Appendix

Book Outline

Chapter 1: What This Rest Contains

    A. A perfect end

        1. Freedom from sin and evil

        2. Personal perfection of body and soul

        3. Our deepest enjoyment of God

    B. Perfect capacities

        1. Of our body and soul

        2. Of our memory

    C. Perfect love

        1. God will embrace us in the arms of love

        2. We will be eternally secure in his love

    D. Perfect joy

        1. We will enter into the joy of the Lord

        2. The Father himself will receive us with joy

Chapter 2: The Four Corners of This Portico

    A. Christ's return

        1. It is absurd to think that Christ will abandon us here

        2. He will come again in glory—do not doubt it

        3. Prisoners will be released and enemies vanquished

B. Our resurrection

   1. Why does death matter if resurrection follows?

   2. We will receive a spiritual, imperishable, immortal body

   3. We should triumph in the promises of our resurrection in Scripture

C. Our judgment

   1. Joy for God's people but terror for his enemies

   2. The saints will not be condemned

   3. We need not fear but rejoice

D. Our coronation

Chapter 3: The Excellent Properties of This Rest

A. Our rest is both costly and free

   1. It cost the blood of the Son of God

   2. But it is free to us—his worth, not ours, is the basis of our title

B. Our rest is corporate and immediate

   1. As we have suffered together, so will we rejoice together

   2. We will receive our rest from God and comprehend it perfectly

C. Our rest is seasonable and suitable

   1. After the difficulty of earth, rest will be welcome and seasonable

   2. Rest is suitable to the natures, desires, and necessities of the saints

D. Our rest is perfect and eternal

   1. Our joy will be perfect, fixed, unmixed, and unchanging

   2. Our rest will never end—it is ours forever

Chapter 4: What We Will Rest From

A. Rest from sin

B. Rest from suffering

1. Rest from all perplexing doubts and fears

2. Rest from all sense of God's displeasure

3. Rest from all the temptations of Satan

4. Rest from the temptations of the world and the flesh

5. Rest from all abuse and persecution

6. Rest from all our sad divisions and un-Christian quarrels

7. Rest from all sadness at the calamities of others

8. Rest from all our own personal sufferings

9. Rest from all the trouble and pain of duty

10. Rest from all the sadness in our absence from God

Chapter 5: A Multitude of Reasons to Move You

A. Thirty arguments for all to consider

1. Our affections and actions should answer their intended ends

2. Our diligence should answer the greatness of the work

3. We should be diligent, for our time is short

4. Our diligence should answer that of our enemies

5. Our actions should match the talents we have been entrusted with

6. Our actions should answer God's great mercy and the price he paid

7. We owe God our all

8. Making haste now avoids the rod to spur us on

9. It would be a crime to trifle when the angels are sent to help us

10. God's goodness and love is a fundamental Christian doctrine

11. No one can ever do too much of this duty

12. The grace of God spurs us on to diligence and speed

13. Those who trifle will pointlessly lose all their labor

14. We have lost a precious amount of time already

15. We will never need to repent of our labors when in heaven

16. God has said that striving for salvation is the way to heaven

17. All will approve of this way in the end

18. Even the most diligent lament their negligence at their death

19. Many men strive for heaven but miss it for lack of more labor

20. God has said that rest will not be had on easier terms

21. God means what he says and is in good earnest with us

22. As Christ was serious in redeeming us, so should we be serious in seeking salvation

23. The Spirit is serious in urging us on

24. Will we neglect God after he has been so good to us?

25. As our ministers are serious, so should we be serious

26. Creatures serve both God and us, and should we not serve God?

27. The servants of the devil are serious, so how can we be less diligent than they are?

28. We should be more diligent serving God than we were when we served Satan

29. We are diligent enough in the things of little worth

30. Heaven and hell are serious and real

B. Ten questions for further conviction

    1. We are willing to be diligent for mere earthly wealth

    2. We would be diligent if the law punished negligence

    3. We would avoid sin if God punished every infraction now

4. If a dead friend came back from hell, we would heed his warning

5. If this was our last day, we would live seriously

6. If we saw the world consumed in judgment, we would be diligent

7. If we saw most people condemned in the judgment, we would tend to our duty

8. If we saw the damned in hell, we would live carefully

9. Imagine how we would live if we were in hell for even an hour and God gave us a second chance

10. Imagine how we would live if we were in heaven for a year and God returned us to the world

C. Ten questions for the godly

1. How should we live in light of the blessings of God?

2. We have felt the pain of our former negligence, so why be negligent now?

3. We have confessed our negligence, so why persist in it?

4. We should keep our covenants with the Lord

5. Should God's own children neglect him?

6. We have tasted such sweetness in duty, so why neglect it?

7. Our uncertainty of our salvation should make us careful

8. If we stand still, we will rapidly go backward

9. We are an example to many, so we should live diligently

10. We represent God to others, so we should live carefully

Chapter 6: Why Are We So Reluctant to Die?

A. Correcting our expectations of rest on earth

1. It is gross idolatry to make any creature or means our rest

2. We contradict the end God has for his gifts and mercies

3. It would be our greatest affliction if earth only was our rest

B. Reproving our unwillingness to die

1. It betrays our doubt about the reality of heaven

2. It reveals the coldness of our love

3. It shows we are not yet weary of sinning

4. It wrongs the Lord and disgraces him in the eyes of the world

5. It shows that we have ignored his many warnings of our death

Chapter 7: The Heavenly Christian Is the Lively Christian

A. Abundant in joy and secure in temptation

1. A heavenly mind is a joyful mind

2. God works on our affections through our mind

3. A heavenly mind will keep our heart employed

4. It will give us a lively view of heaven

5. It will afford us God's protection

B. Lively, patient, and profitable

1. A heavenly mind will put life into all our duties

2. It will sustain us during our afflictions

3. It will make us a profitable Christian to others

C. Honoring to God

D. The cost of neglecting a heavenly life

1. We disobey God's commands

2. We lose the comfort of his most precious promises

3. We frustrate Christ's preparations for our joy

E. The appropriateness of a heavenly life

1. God sets his heart on us; will we not set our heart on him?

2. Heaven, not earth, is our true home and hope

3. There is nothing else worthy of our heart

Chapter 8: Dangerous Hindrances and Positive Helps

A. Seven hindrances to a heavenly life

1. Living in a known sin

2. An earthly mind

3. The company of ungodly and sensual men

4. Frequent disputes about lesser truths

5. A proud and lofty spirit

6. Willful laziness of spirit

7. Contenting ourselves with mere preparation

B. Ten helps to a heavenly life

1. Labor to know heaven as your only treasure

2. Do not rest until you can call this rest your own

3. Labor to apprehend how near your rest is

4. Talk about rest often, especially with those who know it well

5. In every duty wind up your affections nearer heaven

6. Use daily events to remind your soul of its approaching rest

7. Be much in that angelic work of praise

8. Keep your soul with believing thoughts of the love of God

9. Be careful observers of the movements of the Spirit

10. Do not neglect to care for your body

Chapter 9: I Now Proceed to Direct You in the Work

A. The definition of meditation

1. It is set and solemn, constant and regular

2. It is the acting of all the powers of the soul

3. It is not a bare thinking on truths

4. Its object is our everlasting rest

B. The fittest time and place for meditation

1. Determine a set time

2. Meditating frequently will make us familiar, skillful, and warm

3. Choose a seasonable time, both daily and occasional

4. Choose the fittest place

C. Preparing your heart for meditation

1. Put aside all other concerns as far as possible

2. Approach the work with the greatest seriousness

3. Consider the blessed fruit of the work if it succeeds

Chapter 10: How to Fire Your Heart by the Help of Your Head

A. Employing our minds

1. Consideration opens the door between the head and the heart

2. Consideration is reasoning with ourselves using God's arguments

3. Consideration awakens reason from its sleep

B. Stirring our affections

1. Fetch heavenly doctrines from our memory

2. Present those doctrines to our judgment

3. Exercise our belief in the truth of our rest

C. Affections to be stirred

1. Love

2. Desire

3. Hope

4. Courage

5. Joy

Chapter 11: The Most Difficult Part of the Work

  A. Using our senses to aid our faith

    1. Faith is hard; sense is easy

    2. So we should make use of our senses

    3. An example: imagining our future condition

  B. Comparing objects of sense with objects of faith

    1. Compare the delights of saints with the delights of sinners

    2. Compare the delights above with our proper delights here

    3. Compare the excellence of heaven with the works of creation

    4. Compare the deliverance of heaven with God's providence on earth

    5. Compare the mercies of heaven with God's providence on earth

    6. Compare the comforts above with God's supports here below

    7. Compare the glory of heaven with the glory of the church

    8. Compare the glorious change then with the gracious change that the Spirit has already wrought in us here

  C. Managing our hearts

    1. Be aware: our heart will be backward to the work

    2. It will try to deceive us by trifling away the time

    3. It will be easily distracted

    4. It will try to finish the work before it is done

Chapter 12: Preaching to Oneself

  A. The place of soliloquy

  B. Speaking to one's own heart

  C. Stirring love

D. Stirring joy

E. Stirring desire

F. Stirring hope

G. A concluding prayer

Conclusion

A. The change that heavenly meditation brings about

B. But few Christians practice meditation

C. Will we resolve on this heavenly course or not?

General Index

Scripture Index